PRIMARY SCHOOL TEACHERS IN TRIBAL AREAS

By

Dr. Nibedita Priyadarshani
Assistant Professor (Education)
Govt. P.G College
Gopeshwar, (Uttarakhand)
(India)

DISCOVERY PUBLISHING HOUSE PVT. LTD.
NEW DELHI-110 002

Published by:
Tilak Wasan

DISCOVERY PUBLISHING HOUSE PVT. LTD.
4383/4A, Ansari Road, Darya Ganj
New Delhi-110 002 (India)
Phone : +91-11-23279245, 43596064-65
Fax : +91-11-23253475
E-mail : parul.wasan@gmail.com
discoverypublishinghouse@gmail.com
web : www.discoverypublishinggroup.com

***First Edition:* 2012**
ISBN: 978-93-5056-114-0

Primary School Teachers in Tribal Areas

Printed at:
Shree Balaji Art Press
Delhi

Preface

Education is the basic necessity like food, clothes and shelter. But India is lagging behind to provide this basic necessity in spite of its efforts. The literacy rate in most states has not been found satisfactory even after five decades since independence. The situation is worse in tribal areas. Although the number of primary schools has increased 2.82 times since 1951 and enrolments have improved, yet the responsibility of the government by creating a satisfactory infrastructure has in practice not been matched by corresponding outlays. Primary education in India is not only suffering from inadequate allocation of resources but there is also lacking proper management and organization. Teachers are much maligned but not much attention has been given in research to the status and role, the concerns and anxieties, the satisfaction and dissatisfactions of Indian teachers in the face of growing criticism, social pressure and poor economic returns. In the face of growing public criticism, there is a need to try to understand why young enthusiastic teachers turn into bored and aloof professionals in a few years time, why many of our teachers are apathetic and uninvolved and make no effort to improve their scholarship while some others placed in the same milieu are enthusiastic, committed and show a constant desire to grow professionally. We should be concerned about the potential consequences that declining public confidence in education in general and the teaching community in particular may have on the self-esteem and the professional self-image of the teachers.

There are few professions like teaching that are open to intense public scrutiny because most of the schools are maintained by public money, funds from Central, State or Local Government, religious bodies or charitable organizations. There is also a constant flow of information from students to their parents, more so in urban areas, where parents themselves are likely to be educated and more concerned about the education of their wards.

It has been estimated that teachers typically make more than four hundred decisions a day. They dispense acceptance, rejection, praise and reproof on a whole scale basis. Many occupations or professions are distinct on this point from teaching. It is sobering to think that any one of these decisions may have either a short or long-range positive or negative influence upon a given student.

Teachers in India are increasingly facing a condescending attitude from both pupils and parents in rural, urban and tribal areas. That is why the investigator was anxious to investigate stress in teaching—what are the determinants of occupational stress, why teachers are not satisfied with their job, why teachers are not committed to their occupation. This is a matter of great concern as the teacher is the centre of the grand opera of teaching learning and the whole system revolves around him.

Primary school teachers particularly in tribal areas face a lot of stresses in teaching. In tribal areas, there are many factors like poor facilities, lack of advancement, uncongenial working conditions, handling disinterested students, local language barriers etc. Due to these stresses, teachers want to migrate from tribal areas to other areas, take leave showing false reasons and moreover, irregular attendance of the teachers is seen in many schools. That is why author wants to get answers to the following questions especially related to teachers working in tribal areas:

1. Do the teachers face stress in teaching?
2. Are the teachers satisfied with their occupation?
3. Are the teachers committed to their profession?

This book consists of seven chapters. The introductory chapter deals with Occupational Stress, Job-satisfaction and Professional Commitment-concept, genesis, need and importance, objectives and present status. It also discusses the factors of creating stress in teachers, factors of professional commitment and situation of tribal areas.

The various studies related to Occupational Stress, Job-satisfaction and Professional Commitment are presented in the second chapter. The literature under different headings presented are: Studies relating to Occupational Stress, Studies relating to Job-satisfaction and Studies relating to Professional Commitment. The third chapter deals with the problem of the study with rationale and operational definitions. Further, objectives, hypothesis and scope of the study are also highlighted in the study.

The Methodology chapter discusses the design of the study and tools. As the field is in Indian context, the tools required to test the Occupational Stress, Job-satisfaction and Professional Commitment. This chapter also discusses details of the participants, data collection procedure and statistical techniques used in the study. The Analysis and Interpretation chapter discusses the statistical techniques used, nature of data, advantages of ANOVA, basic assumption of ANOVA and mean differences factors like occupational stress, job satisfaction, professional commitment and independent variables like Sex, Socio-economic status, teaching Experience, Length of Service in Tribal Areas and Family size.

The 'Main Findings' chapter presents the analysis and interpretation of data according to the factors like Occupational Stress, Job-satisfaction, Professional Commitment and independent variables like Sex, Socio-economic status, teaching experience, length of service in tribal areas, Family size. As a whole the inter-correlation effect among Occupational Stress, Job-satisfaction and Professional Commitment.

The 'Summary' chapter gives a note of the conclusion on the basis of the findings, educational implications and limitations of the study suggesting further research to be taken in the field of Occupational Stress, Job-satisfaction and Professional Commitment.

This book is a resource book for students, researchers, teachers and the workers working in the field of teacher education.

This work is a fruitful experience of the guidance rendered by Prof. (Dr.) S. M. Gupta, (Retd.)Dean, Faculty of Education, Kurukshetra University, Kurukshetra, Haryana. I acknowledge the generosity of the Headmasters of different High Schools, the teachers who have extended their active cooperation in collecting the data required for the study.

Author

Contents

1

Introduction

The development of a country largely depends on skilled, efficient, trained as well as educated human resources than enriched physical resources. Human resources can be made efficient and intelligent through education. In the ladder of education, primary education plays a vital role. It forms a sound base for secondary and higher education. This is also true with comprehensive development of the individuals. J. P. Naik, an eminent educationist of India, has very aptly observed that the progress of primary education is an index of the general social and economic development of the country as a whole.

Keeping in view the importance of education, the government had introduced the Constitution of 93rd Amendment Bill, 2001 in Parliament to make free and compulsory elementary education for children of the age of 6-14 years a fundamental right. Earlier, the United Front Government had introduced the Constitution (83rd) Amendment Bill, 1997 on the same subject. The parliamentary standing committee had scrutinised the bill and made its recommendations. The directive principles also provide for free and compulsory education of children. Article 45 states that the "State shall endeavour to provide, within a period of 10 years from the commencement of this constitution, for free and compulsory education for all children until they complete the age at 14 years." To make it fruitful, a number of committees have been framed, a number of official resolutions have been adopted and judgments pronounced on various occasions to ensure education for all Indian children. Still the goal of Universal Elementary Education (UEE) remains elusive [Godbole, 2001]. The National Policy on Education (NPE), 1986 as modified in 1992, meticulously enumerated the problems relating to universal elementary education in India [Government of India-1992]. The document not only talks of problems but also recommends several innovative parallel systems to reach the goal of UEE. These innovations no doubt have helped to improve coverage [Chen, 2002], yet a huge gap still exits. According to Amartya Sen, "Primary education in India suffers not only from inadequate allocation of resources, but often enough also, from terrible management and organization problems" [Sen 2002]. To him 'Organization and governance of primary schools has remained neglected subject in much of India'.

Many developing countries have achieved better outcomes while spending far less. India's problem is not insufficient spending but wasteful spending. India currently spends 4.1 per cent of GDP on education and has only 65 per cent literacy. But China spends only 2.2 per cent of GDP on education yet has 91 per cent literacy. Some other countries expenses of GDP on education is given in the table 1.1.

Table 1.1 : Expenses on Education and Literacy Rate

Country	Public Education Expenses/ GDP (in per cent)	Over-15 Literacy rate (in per cent)
India	4.1	65.0
China	2.2	91.0
Indonesia	1.3	88.0
Sri Lanka	1.3	92.5
Vietnam	2.8	90.5
S.Korea	3.6	N.A
UK	4.4	N.A
USA	4.9	N.A

Source: World Development Indicators, 2004

From this table it is a pertinent fact that by international norms India already spends a high proportion of funds on education. Thus, India's problem is not lack of money but lack of quality. Teachers in governmental schools earn twice or thrice the salary of private teachers, yet are unmotivated, skip school and teach very little .One survey by Pratichi in selected West Bengal schools to everyone's surprise showed that only 7 per cent of students could write their own names.

One consequence of it is a very high drop out rate which represents wasted education spending. The proportion of Indian school children who complete class 5 is 59 per cent. It is higher even in Bangladesh (65%) and far higher in Vietnam (85%) or Indonesia (89.5%). Children, who do not complete class V, tend to laps back into illiteracy.

The standard of education in India, as in any other country, depends above all other things on the quality and competence of teachers. Whatever means are adopted for improving education; nothing can be achieved if the concerned teachers do not possess the necessary intellectual and professional abilities. It is obvious that teacher is the heart of every educational institution and the success of an institution in the attainment of educational goals depends largely on the quality and competence of its teachers. Kothari Commission (1964-66) in its report stated that, "If change in a grand scale is to be achieved without violent revolution, (and even then it would still be necessary), there is one instrument, and one instrument only, that can be used: Education... The national system of education is the only instrument that can reach all the people...... It is a difficult instrument, whose effective use requires strength of will, dedicated work and sacrifice. But it is a sure and tried instrument, which has served well other countries in their struggle for development. It can give the will and skill, to do so for India''. In fact, the teacher is the most significant feature in the learning environment provided by the institution. Mishra (1993) rightly stated, "He is not merely an actor on the dias of his classroom, a helper in the practical laboratory, an evaluator of students' multidimensional development, a director of students' learning and social activities, an advisor in moments of personal agony and conflicts, a natural and moral leader of students, a creator of learning climate and instructional material and an able administrator and task mater. His job is noblest in the world and not merely salaried job". To make education an effective and successful instrument of social change and development, there is need of dedicated and committed teachers. Every commission has examined the educational problems of the country and has drawn pointed attention to the teacher's role. The Secondary Education Commission (1952) said, "The reputation of a school and its influence on the life of the community invariably depends on the kind of teachers working in it. Priority of consideration must, therefore, be given to the various problems connected with the improvement of their status."

A teacher plays a predominant part at the elementary school level. Effective teachers are needed in the classroom because even the best curriculum and the most perfect syllabus remain ineffective in the absence of a good teacher. The effectiveness of a teacher is considered to be associated with his personality and mental health. In order to perform his role of paramount and vital significance effectively, a teacher should be an emotionally and professionally satisfied person and free from stress.

The feeling of job-satisfaction and commitment to profession not only enhances efficiency, thinking and emotional reactions-the totality of behaviour but also affects the whole teaching learning process. So, it is pertinent to know about occupational stress, job satisfaction and professional commitment among primary school teachers.

The Tribal

According to the 1991 Census, the population of scheduled tribes in the country is 67.8 million i.e. 8.1 per cent of the total population and is estimated at approximately 88.8 million by 2001, representing 8.6 per cent of the country's total population. Nearly 1/3 rd of the tribal population of the country is found in the states of Madhya Pradesh and Orissa. The ministry of Tribal Affairs was set up in October 1999 for the overall policy planning and coordination of programmes for the development of schedule tribes, scheduled areas (V and VI scheduled) scheduling and rescheduling of tribes, as also the promotion of voluntary efforts in tribal development. The tribal development initiatives focus on areas such as income generation, infrastructure development in tribal areas, educational development, employment oriented training, etc. The Annual plan (2002-2003) emphasizes educational development of scheduled tribes (STs) through many multiple support schemes for improving the enrolment ratio as well as retention of ST students. However, whatever may be the programmes and schemes implemented by the government but fruitfulness of those programmes entirely depend on efficiency of the teachers.

Tribal people are the part and parcel of disadvantaged section of our society, which from the oldest ethnological sector of the population some how referring to the term 'adivasi' which means the original inhabitants of the land. The tribe is a social group of a simple kind, the members of which speaks a common dialect, have a single government, act together for common purpose and have a common name, a contagious territory, a relatively uniform culture or a way of life and a tradition of common descent. Here, the tribe is considered as a social group with common dialect, purpose, name and culture. Bardhan (1973) defines a tribe as a "Course of a socio-cultural entity at a definite historical stage of development. It is a single endogamous community, with a cultural and psychological make up going back into a distant historical past." So, it gives emphasis on their cultural and psychological make up.

From these definitions, it can be concluded that the tribal are the earliest inhabitants having common dialect (though every community has not developed its own language), common culture, who are considered to be out of the main civilized society and who have no religion so to say nor any philosophy of life as others have.

Orissa has a high percentage of S.C. and ST population, which together make approximately 1/3rd of the entire population. The development of SC and ST population has not been remarkable despite the developmental inputs of the state and Central governments. The main thrusts of the socio-economic programmes have not percolated to the grass-root level because of low literacy and poverty. Therefore, educational inputs would go a long way for the overall prosperity of the state.

Occupational Stress

Stress becomes an inevitable fact of life all over the world in the twentieth century due to our ever-changing materialistic life styles. In everyone's life, stress starts from early part of life and continues till death. Everyone experiences it to a more or less extent. So, the natural question is—What is stress?

Compared to other fields of scientific inquiry, the study of occupational stress is relatively new. In fact, the earliest work related to stress could be traced back to the pioneering work of the physiologist, Walter Cannon in the early part of twentieth century (Cannon, 1914) and his investigations of the relationship between emotional and physiological responses. The actual investigation of stress goes back only 50 years to the work of Hans Selye (1956), who is generally regarded as the 'Father of Stress.' The first major programme of research investigating stress in organizations was undertaken at the University of Michigan's Institute for Social Research in the early 1960. Terry Beehr and John Newman's scholarly work on comprehensive review and analysis of the occupational stress literature, gave ground for issue worthy of research attention on occupational stress in the organizational sciences and understanding the meaning of occupational stress.

The word stress is derived from the Latin word 'Strictus', which means, 'to tighten'. This is appropriate when one thinks of the feelings that often accompany stressful situations. When used in occupational stress research, the word stress can be defined in one of three ways. A stimulus definition implied that stress refers to those stimuli in the environment that may require some adaptive response on the part of an employee (i.e. "John has a lot of stress in his job lately"). In contrast, a response definition implies that stress refers to the feelings that one experiences when the demands of the job exceed one's ability to cope (i.e. "John is feeling a lot of stress lately because of deadlines")

However, in contrast to both stimulus and response definitions, a stimulus-response definition implies that 'stress' refers to the overall process by which job demands impact on employees. This process is depicted in Figure 1.1.

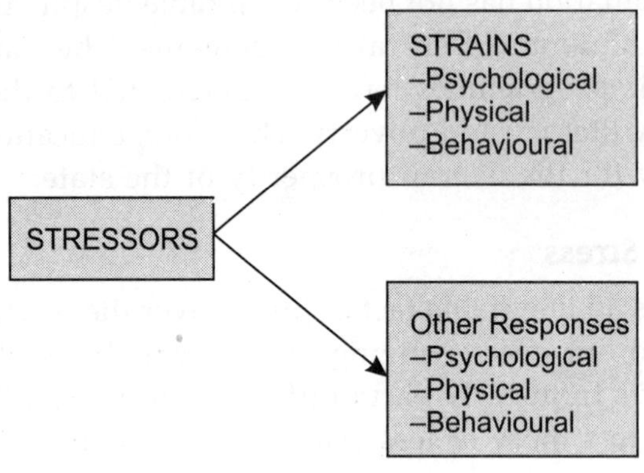

Fig. 1.1

Figure 1.1 The Basic Process by which stressors may lead to strains and other responses.

When this definition is used, the term stressor is used to indicate job or organizational conditions that may require adaptive responses from employees and strain is used to refer to a multiple of negative ways employees may respond when faced with stressors. If an employee's response to a stress were neutral or even positive (Payne, Jabri & Pearson, 1988), such a response would not be considered a strain.

Strains are generally classified as psychological, physical or behavioural. Examples of commonly studied psychological strains include such things as job dissatisfaction, anxiety and depressed mood. Physical strains cover a broad spectrum ranging from minor somatic complaints (e.g. headaches, migraines, change in metabolism, high blood pressure, recurrent viral infections, stomach ulcers, sleep difficulties, upset stomach) to more serious conditions such as coronary heart disease. However, there is no consistent evidence for establishing an objective relationship between occupational stress and physiological health (Berry, 1997; Everly, 1998; Woodbridge, 1998). Finally, behavioural strains include such things as absenteeism, poor performance and turnover.

McGrath (1976) stated that, "By occupational stress is a meant negative environmental factor or stressors associated with a particular job." Suraman and Alutto (1981) stated that "Job demands, constraints and job related events or situations were not in themselves stressful but that they may be capable of producing psychological stress and strain, depending upon personal attributes and other factors."

Though everyone's usual reaction to stress is negative but stress can be a beneficial and positive catalyst in one's life. Selye differentiates stress as positive, Eustress, the factor necessary for one to perform well, particularly under pressure and distress; negative stress which is experienced by an individual when he fails to achieve. Negative stresses like feelings of insecurity, helplessness and desperation obstruct the path of progress and achievement.

Occupational Stress Models

Many occupational researchers have put forth 'models' of the process by which stress in the work environment impact employees. Models are useful primarily because they allow researchers put their findings into some meaningful context. Some models are described in below:

(*a*) Model of work stress

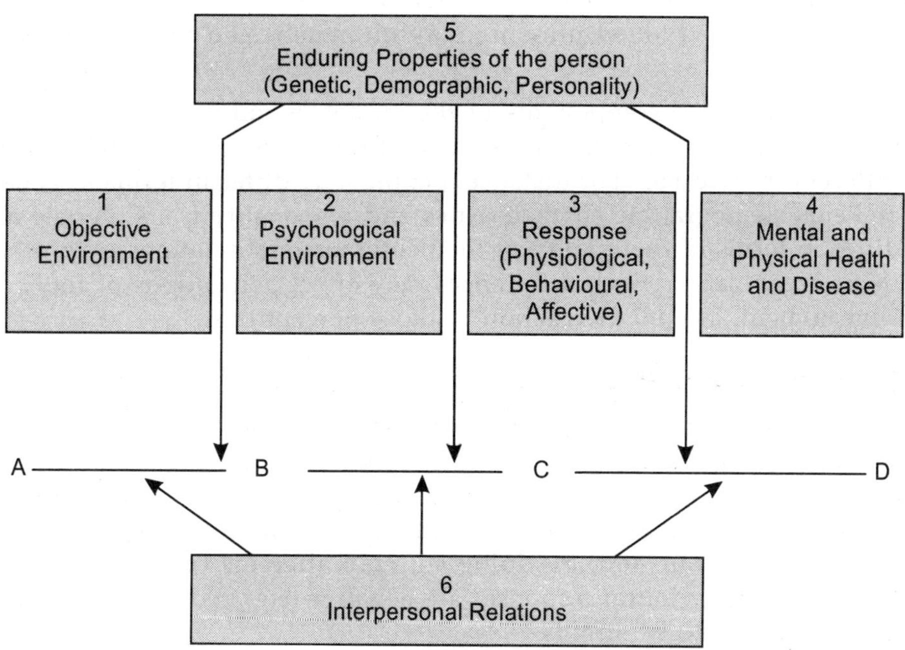

Source: From, D & K Khan, R.L. (1978) The Social Psychology of Organizations (2en ed.) New York: John Wily. Reprinted by permission of John Wiley & Son, Inc.

Fig. 1.2 : ISR Model of work stress

This is the first model of occupational stress prepared by Institute of Social Research at the University of Michigan (French & Kahn, 1962; Kartz &Kahn, 1978). It begins with the objective environment. This includes anything in the organizational environment that may be perceived by employees; for instance, the arrangement of the desks in an office is a part of the objective environment. The second step in this model, psychological environment. This step represents the process by which individuals perceive the objective environment. That is, employees make some appraisal of the objective environment. There may be immediate physiological, behavioural and affective responses on the part of the employee after the environment is appraised. Physiological responses may may include increased heart rate and blood pressure. Behavioural responses may include decreased effort and withdrawal from the workplace. Affective responses may include reduced levels of job satisfaction and increases in depressive symptoms. Depending on the nature of the physiological, behavioural or affective responses to the environment, there may be adverse changes in mental and physical health, as well as disease. Such changes would be considered 'strains', according to this model. For example, physiological changes such as increased heart rate and elevated blood pressure may ultimately lead to coronary heart disease (CHD).

The other two components of the model (5 and 6) describe the fact that the processes depicted in the rest of the model may be different for different individuals. For instance, people may differ in terms of genetic makeup, demographic characteristics and personality traits. People also differ in terms of the quality of their interpersonal relations with others in an organization. Such differences may affect perceptions of the work environment, as well as reaction to those perceptions.

McGrath's Process Model

McGrath conceptualized organizational stress as a four-stage, closed-loop process. The first stage represents situations that employees encounter in organizations. These situations are then perceived via the appraisal process. Once a situation is appraised, individuals then engage in some form of behaviour and, by doing so, may alter the original situation. When such behavioural responses are negative (e.g., reduced effort), they are considered to be strains.

This model indicates us that when employees perceive a stressor in the work environment, they may decide to engage in behaviours that detract from their job performance. For instance, an employee confronted with an unsafe work environment may perceive this to be a stressor. The employee may therefore decide not to put forth as much effort on the job. If this employee ultimately does withhold effort, this will likely reduce his or her job performance.

Teacher Stress

As already discussed, the occupational stress may be due to conflicting demands from others or work overload or work too great relative to the person's perceived capacity. Stress may occur when the worker doesn't fit the job very well or job involves insecurity. Most of the stress is perceived in bureaucratic set up, intense inter-personal relationships, time space restrictions and constant evaluation of effort. However, school is also considered as a major source of stress in the lives of both students and teachers. That many students dropout or fail and many teachers burn out is the evidence that the situation is not right for everyone. Kyria Cou and Sutcliffe (1977, 1978) have defined teacher's stress as a response syndrome of negative aspects (such as anxiety, anger or depression) arising from aspects of the teacher's job and mediated by the perception that the demands made upon the teacher constitute a threat to his self-esteem or well-being and by coping mechanisms activated to reduce the perceived threat.

Some of the studies identified the sources of teacher's stress (Kyriacou, 1987, Laughlin 1984; Dewe, 1986) as follow:

- Poor motivation in pupils
- Pupil indiscipline
- Poor working conditions
- Time pressures
- Low status
- Conflict with colleagues

Pupils' poor attitudes towards school and their lack of motivation, has consistently been identified as a major source of stress in numerous studies (e.g. Laughlin, 1984; Payne and Furnham, 1987). Indeed, it is probably the effort involved in teaching such pupils on a regular basis that forms the single most important source of stress. While actual indiscipline is also a major area of stress, indiscipline by pupils can be dealt with competently by most teachers most of the time without undue stress, (obviously in some schools and for some teachers this may not be the case); the problem of poorly motivated pupils, however, is a more consistent and in some ways harder state of affairs to deal with.

Indiscipline as a source of stress has been widely discussed (e.g. Dunham, 1984; Galloway et al., 1982; Laslett and Smith, 1984). Particular attention has been paid to the way in which a tense and highly unpleasant exchange between a teacher and a pupil can take place almost before the participants have realized how the situation arose. Such exchanges can be extremely stressful at the time, although in most cases they are quickly over.

Poor working condition include such problems as inadequate equipment, poor staffroom facilities and teaching at a split-site school (e.g. Dewe, 1986; Dunham, 1984; Kyriacou and Sutcliffe, 1978b). Time pressures refers to the general level of demands made on teachers within very short periods of time; indeed. The variety of demands made on a teacher in a typical school day, often with tight deadlines attached to them make this aspect of teaching a major area of stress (e.g. Dewe, 1986; Laughlin, 1984).

Low status refers to teachers' perceptions that their profession is held in low esteem by the wider society; this is in part reflected by the level of salaries for teachers and how teaching is discussed by the wider society, particularly through the media. In the United Kingdom, there is little doubt that the recent pay dispute and the criticism of teachers in some newspapers contributed to lowered morale within the profession. This is of great concern, since professional self esteem appears to act as a buffer between stress at work and the likelihood of a precipitating stress-related illness. Some recent studies have indicated that undermining teachers' professional self esteem and identity makes teachers much more vulnerable to teacher burnout (e.g. Kremer and Hofman, 1985).

Conflict with colleagues has also been reported as a major area of stress (e.g. Dewe, 1986; Moracco et al., 1982). Such conflict can range from purely academic disagreements to those arising from the exercise of managerial direction. In the close-knit world of schools, such conflicts can easily escalate if not dealt with skillfully.

While these six areas have emerged as the most commonly identified sources of stress, a number of important caveats need to be borne in mind. *First*, for any individual teacher, almost any aspect of his/her work may result in extreme stress, even if that particular source of stress in general, it is important not to lose sight of individual teacher's concerns (Kyriacou, 1986).

Secondly, there are many changes taking place in schools, so that our understanding of the current major sources of stress needs to be based on up-to-date information. In the United Kingdom, for example, recent changes in the school curriculum (ranging from introducing more science in primary schools to new forms of assessment in the secondary schools) make it very likely that meeting the demands stemming from curriculum changes will emerge as a major stress in schools. In addition, there are areas of major stress which appeared in a number of studies, but not consistently so; of these, the most important appear to be the lack of promotion opportunities, the need to maintain standards, pressure from parents, covering for absent colleagues and being involved in the reorganization of schools.

Thirdly, there are particular groups of teachers which can usefully be looked at separately in order to gain additional insights into their sources of stress. For example, studies of those in managerial positions such as heads of departments (Dunham, 1984), deputy heads (Knutton and Mycroft, 1986) and head teachers (Dunham, 1984), have highlighted the stress stemming from their managerial role: role conflict, motivating colleagues, fears of being unpopular, the exercise of responsibility and difficulties over administrative work. Studies of teachers concerned directly with pastoral care (e.g. Freeman, 1987) have highlighted the difficulties of discharging their role to their own satisfaction, in part because of the nature of trying to help pupils with problems and in part because such teachers have to discharge this role alongside other teaching demands. Studies of student teachers (e.g., Hart, 1987) typically highlighted the concerns over the adequacy of their classroom teaching (both in terms of academic content and in terms of maintaining discipline) and the process of being evaluated by their college supervisor. While a number of studies have presented data focussing on primary schools (e.g., Galloway et al., 1987), secondary schools (e.g. Payne and Furnham, 1987) and special school (e.g. Pont and Reid, 1985), surprisingly few differences in the major types of stress have emerged from comparing teachers in these three groups.

Why do Teachers Experience Stress?

Stress is primarily the body's natural emotional and physiological reaction to the perception of danger in one's environment; in classic psychological terms, the body is being prepared for 'fight' or 'flight'. What is evident now is that such a perception of danger is by no means limited to physical danger, as it presumably was in early evolution. Rather, the perception of threat to one's self-esteem and mental well-being in general is also a potent trigger of this emotional state. Teachers are faced daily with many and various demands; if the teacher perceives that meeting certain demands will be difficult or impossible and that failure to do so will threaten his mental or physical well-being, then the teacher is very likely to experience stress. It is worth noting that such demands may well be self imposed as well as imposed by others just as the judgements about meeting the demands successfully may be based on the teacher's own criteria as well as those of others.

Almost all models of teacher stress acknowledge the central role of the teacher's perception of his circumstances as the trigger for stress (e.g. Payne and Fletcher, 1983; Tellenback et al., 1983), and this goes some way to explaining why teachers in apparently similar circumstances appear to experience different levels of stress. Presumably, those teachers who perceive the circumstances as more threatening are the teachers who experience greater levels of stress. In one sense, stress is in the eye of the beholder. This is of course not to say that an objective assessment of the level of difficulty facing a particular teacher is neither here nor there, but merely to clarify why the nature and type of job demands are not the sole unequivocal predictors of the level of stress the teacher will experience.

Meeting job demands is very dependent on the skills and strategies teachers have and the degree of control they thereby have in dealing with their circumstances. Much research shows that the degree of control teachers feel they have over the demands made upon them and over the frequency and nature of the demands made upon them and over the ability to deal successfully with these demands, stress is likely to be minimized. There is evidence that teachers with a personality disposition to see their life circumstances as in general being under their control are also less likely to experience stress (Kyriacou and Sutcliffe, 1979; McIntyre, 1984)

The major concern with teacher stress in schools is that a prolonged experience of stress can precipitate both mental and physical ill-health (Armes, 1985; Kyriacou and Pratt, 1985; Stratford et al. 1986). While there is much evidence that stress at work appears to be implicated in the ill-health of many teachers, the relationship between occupational stress and subsequent ill-health is a complex one.

Teacher stress is also a problem in schools because of its effect on job performance. This can include teacher absences, taken to avoid stress or resulting from stress-precipitated ill-health, a lowered level of job satisfaction and commitment and even an impaired quality of classroom teaching (in the sense that a teacher's rapport and relationship with pupils can easily be adversely affected if the teacher is experiencing a high level of stress). Whereas in the early 1970s much of the concern also focussed on the number of teachers leaving the profession through stress, as employment prospects elsewhere for ex-teachers became more difficult, this trend appears to have led to many teachers remaining in the profession who would in the past have left. Such teachers may be prone to burnout and account for some of the increase in the number of teachers taking early retirement through ill-health.

Sutcliffe and Whitfield (1976), attempted to identify when teachers were making stressful decisions during a lesson by monitoring their heart rate, only to find that their data largely reflected teachers' physical activity. Behavioural measures such as absenteeism, leaving the profession or ill-health are also prone to influence by too many other factors. The link with ill-health is particularly interesting in this respect, in many other professions. It is likely, however, that the periodic school holidays may well enable teachers to recover physically and mentally from periods of stress and thereby mitigate any ill-health that would otherwise have occurred in a way that is not available to those in most professions.

The stressors identified by the National Institute of Occupational Safety and Health as important *psychosocial risk factor (or stressors)* in the workplace (Sauter, Murphy & Hurrell, 1990) are work load and work pace, work schedule, role stressors, career security factors, interpersonal factors, and job context.

Role Stressors

A role can be defined as a set of behaviours that are expected of a person occupying a particular position. Most of us play multiple roles in life (e.g. parents, employee, spouse, community member) and thus have multiple sets of behavioural expectations. In social systems such as organizations roles serve the important function of coordinating individual members' behaviour (Katz & Khan, 1978). Without roles, most organizations would function very poorly or even cease to exist.

Employees in organizations receive role-related information through both formal and informal sources. The most typical formal sources of role-related information are written job descriptions and communication with immediate supervisors. The information gleaned from these information sources, however, does not completely define an employee's role. For example, many readers will actually do on their job. This is because there are many other sources of role-related information, including subordinates, co-workers at the same level and even customers. The term role set is used to denote the various sources that communicate role-related information to employees.

Ideally, role-related information is clearly communicated to employees and the members of a role set provide consistent information. Unfortunately, this does not always happen. When role-related information is clearly communicated to employees and the members of a role set provide consistent information. Unfortunately, this does not always happen. When role-related information is unclear, this may lead to a stressor known as role ambiguity (King & King, 1990; Kahn et al., 1964).

To appreciate fully the nature of role ambiguity, it is useful to think about starting a new job. Those who have recently gone through this experience would likely attest to the fact that this is a time of considerable uncertainly that, for most people, is stressful (Beehr & Bhagat, 1985).Fortunately, the stress associated with starting a new job is tempered by the fact that the performance expectations for brand-new guity is a consistent feature of their jobs.

Role ambiguity may occur for a number of reasons. First, organizations may simply be lax in revising outdated or poorly written job descriptions. Because these job descriptions are often the first source of role-related information for a new employee, this may start the new employee off with a sense of ambiguity and confusion. Second, some roles are simply more difficult to define than others. This is especially true of managerial positions (Campbell, Dunnette, Lawler & Weick, 1970). In many organizations, managers are held accountable for certain results (e.g., achieving a certain level of profitability) but are given very little guidance as to the behaviours required to achieve those results.

A third common cause of role ambiguity is environmental change, because the content of many organizational roles is linked to factors and events outside of the organization. When these change, the requirements of the role often change or become unclear. For example, societal exceptions of educational institutions have changed considerably in recent years. Educational institutions, at all levels, are now expected to shape students' values and attitudes, in addition to providing them with the basic skills needed to become productive members of society. Such changes in societal expectations may lead to considerable role ambiguity on the part of educators; that is, members of this profession may ask themselves questions such as: How far should I go in shaping students' values? What are the 'correct' values to be taught? What is the correct balance between shaping values and teaching basic skills?

The assessment of role ambiguity has been almost exclusively through self-report measures. By far the most widely used measure of role ambiguity has been the scale developed by Rizzo, House and Litzman (1970). A sample item from this scale is, 'I know what my responsibilities are.' If an employee were to disagree strongly with this statement, this would be indicative of role ambiguity. Despite much debate over the years regarding the relative merits of this scale (e.g., Kelloway & Barling, 1990; Netemeyer, Johnston & Burton, 1990; Smith, Tisak & Schmier, 1993; Tracy & Johnson, 1981), there have been efforts to develop alternative measures.

An alternative role ambiguity scale that may prove quite useful to occupational stress researchers was recently developed by Breaugh and

Colihan (1994). One of the nice features of this scale is that it breaks role ambiguity into three dimensions that are represented by three dimensions that are represented by three subscales (Work Method Ambiguity: 'I know how to get my work done', Scheduling Ambiguity: 'I know when I should be doing a particular aspect [part] of my job', and performance criteria Ambiguity: 'I know what my supervisor considers satisfactory work performance'). As with the item from the Rizzo et al (1970) scale, disagreement with it breaks role ambiguity.

Measuring multiple facets of role ambiguity makes sense because this stressor can be manifested in a variety of ways (King & King, 1990). The Breaugh and Colihan scale therefore allows for more precise measurement of role ambiguity. This greater precision than the Rizzo et al. (1970) scale because it helps pinpoint specific ways in which amguity can be reduced (e.g., clarifying performance expectations). Furthermore, in limited use it has been shown to have acceptable measurement properties (Allen & Jex, 1995; Heinisch & Jex, 1996).

Another problem that may occur as employee roles develop is that role-related information provided by one member of a role set may conflict with the information provided by another member. When this happens, the stressor that results is role conflict (Kahn et al., 1964). In occupational stress research, the form of role conflict that is studied most often is intra-role conflict. This simply means that an individual receives conflicting messages pertaining to one role. For example, a salesperson may be told by one manager to spend more time prospecting for new customers whereas another manager may feel more time should be spent providing service to existing customers. This form of role conflict can be distinguished from inter-role conflict, which refers to competing role demands that arise from different role. A very pertinent example of this is the tension that often results from the competing demands of work and family (Frone, Russell & Cooper, 1991). The topic of inter-role conflict will not be covered here, because there are other excellent sources of information about this stressor elsewhere (e.g., Cartwright & Cooper, 1997; Greenhaus &Parasuraman, 1986; Gupta & Jenkins, 1985).

What causes a person to experience role conflict? Most often this is due to poor communication and coordination among role senders (Schaubroeck, Ganster, Sime & Ditman, 1993). In many organizations, information flow is poorly coordinated and as a result, an employee may receive conflicting information from members of his or her role set.

In some cases, however, role conflict is unavoidable because of characteristics inherent in a particular role. Many people occupy what are termed boundary spanning role in organizations (Katz & Kahn, 1978).

Such roles require that an employee frequently interact with and respond to individuals and groups both inside and outside of an organization. Unfortunately, the demands of these various groups and individuals may be conflicting. A good example of a boundary spanning role is that of an elected official in a democratic government. An inherent feature of this role is that the occupant often must balance the competing demands of the electorate and of special interest groups (e.g., corporations, unions, trade associations).

As is the case with role ambiguity, the problem of role conflict may also be intensified by environmental changes. In response to change, organizational roles become more complex, this greatly increases the potential for role conflict. A good example of this is the changing role of coaches in professional sports. In the past, coaches functioned primarily as authority figures and exerted considerable control over players. More recently, due to changing views regarding authority and to escalating salaries, coaching at this level has become much more complex. As a result, coaches must often mediate between the often competing demands of maintaining authority and keeping players happy.

A third role stressor that has been examined in the occupational stress literature is role overload, which is defined by Jones, Flynn and Kelloway (1995) as a stressor that occur when 'an employer may demand more of an employee than he or she can reasonably accomplish in a given time, or simply, the employee may perceive the demands of work as excessive'. To understand role overload, it is useful to distinguish between quantitative and qualitative role overload. When quantitative role overload is experienced, the employee is fully capable of meeting role demands. The problem is simply that there are too many role demands for the employee to handle. Given more time and perhaps resources, the employee who is quantitatively overload could meet his or her role demands. On the other hand, when an employee is quantitatively overloaded, the demands of the role exceed his or her skills and abilities. In this case, even with more time and resources, the employee would not be able to meet his or her role demand.

Even when staffing levels are adequate, employees may still be quantitatively overloaded due to poor job design or poor communication among role senders. Jobs may be designed in a variety of ways, depending on the outcome an organization is trying to maximize employee motivation but it completely ignores efficiency, an employee may be highly motivated yet overloaded. Poor communication among role senders can also result in quantitative role overload in cases in which role demands may be compatible but, taken together are excessive.

Workload

Workload can be defined as simply the amount of work an employee has to do. This definition, however, is deceptively simple for three reasons. First, to truly understand workload, it is necessary to distinguish between perceptions of workload and actual workload. That is two employees may have the same number of task to complete, but one may perceive his or her workload to be higher than the other. Second, for many jobs workload is cyclical. Tax accountants, for example, experience a sharp increase in workload as the deadline for filing tax returns approaches. As McGrath and Beehr (1990) aptly point out, this is true of many other variables in occupational stress research. Unfortunately, in most research, all variables are measured at one point in time so there is no way to assess these cyclical changes. It is necessary to distinguish between the sheer volume of work one is required to perform (quantitative workload) and the difficulty of the work (qualitative workload).

Workload is undoubtedly affected by many of the same factors that impact role overload. Occupational stress researchers typically examine workload as a distinct stressor because it is affected by demands that require no 'role-sending' processes. For example, the workload of a design engineer is likely to be affected by role-related demands from others. On the other hand, such an individual's workload may also be influenced by the inherent complexity of his or her job tasks. This is true of many jobs that require employees to use very high-level mental skills. This is not meant to imply that the relationship between job complexity and strain is necessarily linear (i.e., as complexity increases, stress increases). According to Xie and Johns (1995), for example, jobs are experienced as stressful when they are either very low or very high in complexity. In case of low complexity, the stress may result from boredom, whereas high complexity may lead to mental fatigue and exhaustion. Either way, the result may be negative.

Workload may be measured either subjectively or objectively. Objective workload measures might include hours of work, number of projects, number of clients served or possibly, number of products produced. Objective workload measures are appealing because they do not require any interpretation on the part of employees. Unfortunately, most objective measures are rather crude indicators of workload. Hours of work probably provides the best illustration of this point. Subjective measures are based on employees' perceptions of their level of workload.

Interpersonal Conflict

Most jobs involve some interaction with other people (e.g., co-workers, contractors, customers), and such interactions can be a source of satisfaction and fulfillment (Spector, 1997a). Unfortunately, at times interactions with others can make work more stressful when they result in interpersonal conflict (Keenan & Newton, 1985). The intensity of interpersonal conflict can range from minor disagreements between co-workers to heated arguments. In the extreme, interpersonal conflicts may even lead to physical violence.

Several factors in the workplace may increase the probability of interpersonal conflict. For example, it has been well established in the social psychological literature that competition is often a precursor to conflict. Therefore, two employees may not get along well because they are competing for the same promotion. Competition may also be heightened when employees must compete for scarce organizational resources. In many organizations, the budget allocation process creates what is termed a zero-sum game. That is, the more Department A receives, the less Department B will be allocated. When this is the case, interpersonal conflict is often a by-product.

Interpersonal conflict may also be more likely to occur when an employee feels that he or she is being treated unfairly or unprofessionally by a co-worker. This may be through expressions of rudeness or disrespect. In work groups, such feelings of unfairness may also be engendered by what is termed free riding among group members (Albanese & Van Fleet, 1985; Roberts, 1995). Free riding is simply the tendency on the part of some work group members not to 'pull their weight' which requires the more hardworking group members to pick up the slack. Those picking up the slack may resent the free rider and the result may be interpersonal conflict among group members.

In some work situations, interpersonal conflict may still be present even though conditions that foster competition may be minimal and co-workers treat each other with fairness and respect. In such cases, interpersonal conflict may largely be due to stable individual differences among coworkers. According to Swap and Rubin (1983), some people are naturally more competitive than others. Thus, a group composed of a large number of naturally competitive people may have a high degree of interpersonal conflict, despite favourable situational influences. In cases like this, the best way to minimize interpersonal conflict would possibly be to change the composition of the group.

Situational Constraints

The effectiveness of organizations depends largely on the job performance of individual employees (Cambell, 1990). Thus, it is an organisation's best interest to create organizational conditions that facilitate individual's job performance. Unfortunately, organizations may inadvertendently fail to do this at times. The result is that 'situational constraints' are imposed on employees. Peter and O'Connor (1980) define situational constraints as any conditions in an employee's immediate work environment that inhibit or constrain performance. Situational constraints essentially prevent employees from translating skills, abilities and motivation into high levels of job performance.

Peters and O'Connor (1988) identified 11 primary categories of situational constraints in organizations: (*a*) job-related information, (*b*) budgetary support, (*c*) required support, (*d*) materials and supplies, (*e*) required services and help from others, (*f*) task preparation, (*g*) time availability, (*h*) the work environment, (*i*) scheduling of activities, (*j*) transportation, and (*k*) job-relevant authority. For any of these categories of constraints, the inhibiting effect on performance may be due to unavailability, inadequacy or poor quality.

To illustrate more clearly how situational constraints might inhibit performance, take the example of job-related information. A detective trying to solve a crime may be unable to do so simply because of lacking information. That is, the crime may be unable to do so simply because of lacking information. That is, the criminal may have left no clues, and there are no witnesses. However, it is also possible that clues and witness are available, but they are either inadequate or of poor quality. For example, the detective may receive a tip that the criminal has fled to 'another state' or witnesses may 'think' they spotted the criminal. In both cases, the information may be of some value but, by itself, would probably not lead to the apprehension of the suspect.

When organizations reduce staffing levels, lay off survivors may lose access to needed support personnel and as a result, their performance may suffer. Also, the increasing role demands that often confront layoff survivors may result in less time available for task accomplishment.

Differences were found in role related stress experienced by male versus female schoolteacher's working in general schools as compared to no gender-based difference in teachers working in special schools. Teachers and professors scored high on emotional exhaustion intensity, emotional exhaustion frequency and depersonalization frequency (Joshi & Singhvi, 2000). Differences were found between reported occupational stress among public and private sector by public relation officers. Higher stress was reported by public sector public relation officers (Misra, 1997).Similarly, bankers of non-nationalized banks reported higher stress levels as compared to those of nationalized banks (Amnabhavi & Triveri, 2000).

In comparison of role stress experienced by officers, bankers and schoolteachers, it was found that teachers experienced least role stress (Pereek & Mehta, 1997). Sultana (1995) noted significant differences between both professional male and female teachers on the dimensions of inter-role distance, role stagnation, role erosion, role-overload and role ambiguity. Mishra (1996) reported that female teacher's experienced greater role related stress, personal stress and role overload as compared to their male colleagues. A moderate level of stress was observed among women doctors, teachers, bank officers and bureaucrats (Gaur & Dhawan, 2003). Executives were found to be more stressed than physicians, especially in the area role insufficiency (Ghosh, 2000). University teachers experienced less stress than bank managers (Bankat & Parveen, 1999). Employees of administrative organizations reported greater stress than those working in financial organizations at the same level in the hierarchy (Sahoo, Mohanty & Bhakat, 1995). Nurses perceived more work stress then lectures but did not express more personal strain (Oupen, 1996)

From the above discussion, it is pertinent to say that stress arises when the demand of the environment exceeds the person's capabilities and resources for meeting it. One experiences stress in occupation when job demand constraints. Job-related events or situations produce psychological stress and strains, depending upon personal attributes and other factors like role overload, role ambiguity, role conflict, lack of recognition, low status and poor working conditions etc.

Job-satisfaction

The word 'satisfaction' is derived from Latin word Satis + facet. 'Satis' means enough and facet means to do. So, satisfaction means to do enough. Job occupies an important place in the life of an individual. It is the chief source of satisfaction of an individual's psychological, biological and social needs. Therefore, job-satisfaction has been defined in different ways by many researchers.

According to Longman's Dictionary of Psychology and Psychiatry (1984), job satisfaction is the attitude of a worker towards his job, sometimes expressed as hedonic response of liking or disliking the work itself, the rewards (pay, promotions and recognition, etc.) or the contest (working condition and benefits, etc.).

Job satisfaction is a complex concept. Its definition varies from person to person due to the following reasons:

1. The varied nature of job that an individual performs.
2. Various disciplines like psychology, sociology, education and management have explained this term in a number of ways.

3. Various researchers to study job-satisfaction have used large number of methods.

Hoppick (1935) has brought job-satisfaction into limelight. According to him, job-satisfaction was a combination of psychological, physiological and environmental circumstances that makes a person to say truthfully, 'I am satisfied with my job'. Bullock (1962) stated, 'Job-satisfaction is an attitude which results from balancing and summation of many specific likes, dislikes and experiences in connection with job.'

Barber (1980) described, "Job-satisfaction as the quality, state or level of satisfaction which is the result of various interests and attitudes of a person towards his job." Brayfield and Rothe (1951) state that job satisfaction, refers to how people feel about different jobs. However, a common and generally applicable definition of the term given by Varoom (1964) job satisfaction is a positive orientation of an individual towards work roles which he is presently occupying. Ronan (1970) states that satisfactions are expressed opinions concerning the job, the organization and variables related to job content. Kalleberg (1977) in his definition states job satisfaction refers to an overall affective orientation on the part of individuals towards work roles, which they are presently occupying. But Hackman (1977) defines job satisfaction more precisely refers to a person's affective attitudes or orientation towards a job. It is one measure of the quality of life in organizations. There is an increasing acceptance of the view that material possessions and economic growth do not necessarily produce a high quality of life. Recognition is now being given to the importance of the kind of affective recognitions that people experienced on the job. So, job satisfaction of a worker in his work. It is a source of satisfaction of physical, psychological and social needs of an individual in his work. Therefore, job satisfaction involves dynamic interaction between the individual and the environment.

So, job-satisfaction is the result of various attitudes that a person holds towards his job, towards related factors and towards life in general. It is the direction of life one had adopted. Job-satisfaction is the whole material of job factors that make a person like his work situation and be lead for it without distaste in the beginning of his work. Different educationists, psychologists etc. studied job-satisfaction with different variables. Kolte (1978) studied the job-satisfaction of primary school teachers. It was undertaken to identify the factors that are responsible for both the teachers' satisfaction and dissatisfaction. The study found that achievement, recognition, advancement, work itself, policy and administration, working conditions, salary and interpersonal relations were serving as satisfiers and dissatisfies.

Anbraham (1994) studied, "job-satisfaction and teacher effectiveness" and found that who had a high level of the job-satisfaction were more effective teachers than those with low level of job-satisfaction.

It can be concluded that job-satisfaction is an attitude that results from balancing and summation of many specifics likes dislikes and experiences in connection with job. Working conditions, salary, interpersonal relations, achievement, recognition etc. are some of factors of job-satisfaction.

Professional Commitment

The word commitment has been used in everyday language. But what is its real meaning? Chaucer (1386) stated it as 'entrusting' or giving charge of some responsibility. Afterwards this term has been used to denote various forms of actions and attitudes.

Sociologists use commitment in the analysis of both individual and organizational behaviour. They describe it as forms of action, characteristic of particular kinds of people or groups. They use it as an independent variable to account for certain kinds of behaviour of individuals or groups.

Becker (1960) for the first time explicitly stated meaning and uses of commitment. According to him "One of the outstanding characteristic of commitment is the consistency in the lines of behaviour of the committed people". The committed people remain stick to that line of action, whatever may be the decision regarding a course of action. Such a decision could be taken regarding any ideology, religion, organization, occupation, profession or person. So, committed person shows consistent line of behaviour.

The reason of showing consistent behaviour may be due to social sanction and social control. People act consistently as it is desirable in a society or social group. Some act as they consider it is morally wrong to do otherwise. Thus existence of universally accepted cultural values of a group or society constrain behaviour of its people. Some psychologists stated that people shows consistent behaviour due to stable structure of personal need. All individuals have some stable needs and consistently adhere to a particular course of action in order to maximize the possibilities of satisfying them.

Schelling (1956) advocated the theory of side-bets for the consistency of behaviour on commitment. The major elements of the consistency behaviour are:

1. The individual decides a particular way of behaviour, which is accepted by others or according to the interest of others.

2. He has placed himself in such a position by his own prior actions.
3. The committed persons must be aware that he has made the side-bets and his decision in this case will have ramifications beyond it. From this side-bets theory, the most necessary component of commitment is interest created by one's own prior action.

Some persons may not change their job because their reputation is at stake. If they change the job, they will not be considered trustworthy. Hence, despite of better opportunities he may not leave his present job. There are various side-bets to keep one committed. There may be some benefits in a job, which may not be present in others, so the person never wants to change the profession. In some cases, one is adjusted to a particular way of activities in such a way that he never wants to change that occupation.

Goffman's (1955) analysis of face-to-face interaction is another way in which side-bets are made through operation of social process. According to him, people continue to behave in the same manner for the sake of 'face-saving'.

Backer's thorough analysis also shows that some commitments are made consciously, whereas others arise crescively, the person become aware of his commitment, only at some point of change. He seems to have made commitment without realizing it. Backer termed it as 'commitment by default'. So commitment is maintained mostly due to conscious decision.

Reasons of Commitment

Social control and social sanction: The reason for adherence to a consistence line of behaviour could be many e.g. it could be due to social sanction and social control. People act consistently because activity of some particular kind is regarded as right or proper in a society or social group. Deviation from the standard is punished or disapproved by the social group. People act consistently, because it is morally wrong to do otherwise. Thus existence of universal accepted cultural values of a group or society inform and constrain behaviour of its people.

Stable structure of personal needs: Another reason given by some psychologists for consistency of behaviour is the stable structure of personal needs. They predicate that all individuals have some stable needs and people consistently adhere to a particular course of action in order to maximise the possibilities of satisfying them.

Side-Bets: Schelling (1956) advocated the theory of 'side-bets' for the consistency of behaviour or commitment. According to him, a committed person has, originally, at the time of choosing a line of action, from several alternatives, has acted in such a way, as to involve other interests of his, originally extraneous, to the action he is engaged in. Later on, at another point of time, even if he wishes to change his line of action, the consequences will be so expensive that the alternative course of action, consequences will not be profitable or feasible. The major elements of commitments involved in such behaviour are:

Firstly, the individual is in a position in which his decision with regard to some particular line of action has consequences for other interests; secondly, he has placed himself in such a position by his own prior actions; and thirdly, the committed person must be aware that he has made the side-bets and that his decision in this case will have ramifications beyond it. The element of recognition of the interests created by one's own prior action is a necessary component of commitment.

Side-bates is not always deliberately made by the person himself. Often the person finds that his involvement in social organisations or adherence to a particular line of action has in effect made side-bets for him and thus constrained his future activities. Side-bets occur in several ways.

Generalised Cultural Expectation

One way of side-bets influencing the course of action is the existence of generalised cultural expectations. A person may change his job, because his reputation is at stake. If he changes his job, he will be considered not trustworthy. Hence despite of better opportunities he may not leave his present job.

Operation of Impersonal Bureaucratic Arrangement

Side-bets are also made for a person by the operation of impersonal bureaucratic arrangements, e.g., person who wishes to leave his present job may be unable to do so because by leaving the present job, he will lose considerable sum of money by not getting any pension and other related rules of it, may influence his decision of adhering to his present job.

Constraining Behaviour

Side-bets constraining behaviour also come into operation because individuals adjust to social positions. A person may so alter his pattern of activity in the process of confirming to the requirements for one such position that he unfits himself for other positions. As a nursery teacher may refuse to teach senior classes because she has so adjusted her style of teaching the nursery classes that she no more wishes to radically change her style of teaching and start preparing for senior classes all over again. Any change in her style of teaching will need adjustment to new situations and hamper the case with which she has learnt to handle the nursery classes. Hence, she may refuse to teach the senior classes and adhere to her present job position.

Face to Face Interaction

Goffman's (1995) analysis of face-to-face interaction is another way in which side-bets are made through operation of social process. He points out that, having once claimed to be a certain kind of person, often it becomes necessary for him to behave in conformity with that image. Thus, people continue to behave in the same manner for the sake of 'face-saving' and the rules governing face to face interaction are such that others will ordinarily help the individual in preserving the self image he has been projecting.

Backer's analysis show that some commitments are made crescively, the person becomes aware of his commitment, only at some point of change. He seems to have made commitment without realizing it. Becker termed it as commitment by default. He points out that it arises through a series of acts, no one of which is crucial time of making a decision to change from original line of action that he becomes conscious of the accumulated strength of the side-bets and hence decides to adhere to the original line of activity. Backer concludes that conscious decisions are:

Value Prevalent in a Society

Different cultures, societies and groups have variant sets of values and hence they have different sets of values and hence they have variant sets of valuables on which side-bets can be made. Thus in a society where money is meaningless. Side-bets could be in the form of time, energy and money to achieve a certain goal. All these things are the side-bets which determine his further course of action. Logically therefore, side-bets derive their meaning from the value patterns is necessary in order to understand the concept of commitment. The value pattern of a society is one of the most important elements of commitment.

Commitment is a conscious decision of an individual, supported by side-bets and expressed in the form of consistent line of action or behaviour in a particular value orientation. It refers to an objective reality, which exists beyond normal perception. It represents a mental construct of perceived reality. The mental construct or image of a committed person could be different according to one's own perception of reality. Jean Piage maintains that causation, spatiality and temporality in perception bring out many facts of its existence in the minds. Likewise, commitment has been perceived differently by different social thinkers according to the difference in the reference and the context of their study. Some social thinkers have studied it as a variable, affecting their universe of study, while others have taken it as a phenomena or a mental state, affected by other socio-cultural, economic and physical variables.

In the present study, commitment has been viewed from both points of view. It has been pre-supposed that commitment is a state of mind which positively affects the efficiency of teachers as professionals. It has also been studied as a phenomena or mental attitude of the teachers towards their profession, affected by other variables particularly, the morbidity.

There could be unending debate regarding such questions as; what is commitment? Or who is a committed person? Becker has tried to understand the concept of commitment by analysing one of the several images invoked by the term commitment, in the present study also; an attempt has been made to construct a mental image of an ideally committed teacher. This image does not correspond to any particular individual but it serves the purpose of identifying the indicators of commitment. Through an inductive study of imaginary committed teachers, some indicators of commitment are identified, which constitutes the index of commitment was considered of further utility in measuring the level of professional commitment among teachers and deducing whether or not any particular teacher is professionally committed.

It has been presupposed that a committed teacher is an asset to the school as well as to the teaching profession as a whole; that he/she will have several qualities which will improve the quality of education. A teacher who possesses more or less of these qualities is accordingly graded as more or less committed teacher professionally. It is difficult to describe a committed teacher in one word or in one sentence but generally speaking, in the present study the concept of professionally committed teacher represents, a teacher who is aware of the demands of her profession; one who is sincere in discharging her duties as a teacher; who works in confirmation to the aims and objectives of education; who has in heart, the welfare and progress of the children and the nation as a whole; one who is competent in her subject and makes constant efforts to achieve the goal of good education, is considered a committed teacher.

Stay-back

Stay-back can be defined as the office after that employees stay behind in the office hours, regardless of what they do (Cole, 1979; Sekaran, 1989).

Stay-back was broadly divided into two types, namely voluntary stay-back and compulsory stay-back. Voluntary stay-back happens out of the teachers 'own free will. On the other hand, compulsory stay-back, as the name suggests itself, happens because teachers are required to stay as part of the fulfillment of their official duties. For example, staff meeting, assigned extracurricular activities, assigned counselling work, assigned tutorial classes, on duty. Voluntary stay-back can further be divided into two sub-groups: educational stay-back (counselling, tutorial classes, preparation for lessons, tests, assignments, etc.) and non-educational stay-back (non educational reading, waiting for pick-up, knitting, etc.).

In addition to above factors of professional commitment, Mowday and Mc Dade (1979) gave following factors:

- A strong belief in and acceptance of the profession's goals and values.
- A willingness to exert considerable effort on behalf of the profession.
- A strong desire to maintain membership in the profession.

Numerous studies have suggested that employees' job attitudes and commitment can affect their performance (Cammann et al., 1983; Oldham and Hackman, 1981). For personal factors they include locus of control (Cheng, 1990), age, tenure, gender and education level (Fink, 1992). Non-demographic individual difference variables include central life interest (Dubin et al., 1975), desire for greater job responsibility, expectations about goal achievement and personal needs (Steers, 1977).

For organizational characteristics, they consist of job, leadership, work group and organizational characteristics. Among these four characteristics, leadership and organizational characteristics seem to be of utmost concern to school managers who want to arouse the commitment and enhance the performance of teachers. Leadership refers to the style of the leaders which can be supervisory (Fukami and Larson, 1984), charismatic (Conger et al., 1988), one of initiating structure and consideration (Morris and Sherman, 1981) and one of giving rewards (Bateman and Strasser, 1988). For organizational characteristics, they include things like formalization, decentralization, functional dependence on the work of others and participation in decision making (Morris, Steers and Rhodes, 1978).

Other factors such as lateness, absenteeism, tardiness and turnover are the manifestations of commitment as reflected in most literature. But there is a kind of behaviour which can be a predictor of employees' level of commitment and which has not yet been studied thoroughly. It is "employees' stay-back time after normal office hour". By providing teachers with inspiration, encouragement and more meaning to their work, a charismatic principal can enhance a teacher's faith in and respect for him and these lead to an increase in the teacher's commitment to the principal and so to the school and the work. Additional studies by Cole (1979) and Sekaran (1989) have further reinforced that employees' stay-back is also a manifestation of commitment and can be used as a predictor of commitment-related behaviour mentioned by other researchers. According to Anita Hung and James Liu, stay-back was broadly divided into two types, namely voluntary and compulsory stay-back. Voluntary stay-back happens out of the teachers' own free will. On the other hand, compulsory stay-back., in which teachers is required to stay as part of the fulfillment of their official duties. For example staff meeting, assigned extra curricular activities, detention class, assigned counselling work, assigned tutorial classes, activities on duty, etc. are some of the activities of compulsory stay-back. Voluntary stay-back can further be divided into two sub-groups: educational stay-back and non-educational stay-back.

Areas of Commitment

The major objective of education in the 21st century is identified as social cohesion. The background for this identification can be easily understood on the basis of existing social, cultural and economic realities which invariably give rise to several tensions, crises and avoidable disparities. Competent teachers could certainly respond to most of the issues through their professional expertise and appropriate utilization of relevant competencies. However, within the schools, with parents and also with other members of the community, what would eventually matter is the way they perform their role model.

Only such a person would become a true teacher who sincerely loves each and every child; is open to criticism not only from peers and elders but also from the youngsters; and is truthful in all his actions and deeds. The teachers have to be quite sensitive to emotional needs of children, especially of those who need to be handled with sensitivity and perseverance. Teacher's tolerance, humility and modesty could endear them to their pupils, to the community and the parents alike, thus enhancing their confidence in the total process of education. These qualities along with professional competencies of teachers would ensure their commitment and dedication to the profession at their very best. The following five commitment areas play vital role in shaping the teachers' role performance and building the future citizens of India:

Commitment to the Learner

Learning is an attitude, which starts taking shape at the school and stays throughout life. This is made possible when the learner is a joyful and rewarding experience. It gives joy not only to the learner but also to the teacher who loves and cares for the learner. It is a gratifying experience for a learner to be in secure hands of the teacher. Commitment to the learner implies teachers' genuine love and affection for children, tolerance towards their mistakes and mischief coupled with their pedagogically correct interpretations, commitment to their progress and development, concern for their progress and development, concern for their human empowerment and care for the development of quality of life among the children. These commitments will indeed, add to the effectiveness of every teacher's role performance.

Genuine love for children and tolerance towards the learners can be correlated while teaching educational psychology. The teachers should do self analysis of their own aggressive behaviour and write down their individual experiences in order to understand their reactions and modify their behaviour accordingly. Self-analysis is, in fact, an important tool for commitment building. The teacher should also know about the impact of their intolerance and aggressiveness on the growth and development of the children. They should make sincere efforts for the wholesome development of the children in every respect under their caring guidance. This commitment is quite crucial on the part of the teachers in making the learning effective and as such it ought to be inculcated in them through teacher education programmes.

Commitment to the Society

Teachers are responsible to the local community individually as well as collectively. They must serve it faithfully and conscientiously. This service may be of different types. For instance, those actions of the society who were denied the right to education in the past require special attention and commitment. Similarly, children of the parents coming from the poor and deprived sections too need extraordinary care and love. Encouraging and enthuasing them to join the ranks of the educated will not beneficial to them alone, but also to the society as a whole. Their enhanced knowledge, skills and attitudes will lead to increased productivity to improve the quality of life of the whole community. The adults belonging to this section of the society could be encouraged to join adult education and non-formal education classes while all children of the schools or NFE classes so as to help them get educated to contribute their share in improving the quality of their life as also that of the community. Teacher's commitment to the community may basically relate to developing the sense of equality for children of the poor and illiterate parents, willingness to take initiative to advise the parents for enrichment of the child and community mobilisation for development of the school; and willingness to actively participate in the enrolment drive.

The teacher who is committed to the society would very soon create a sense of belonging among its members. Once this is achieved, there would not be any problem in mobilising the community for raising resources for the school in terms of physical facilities or for encouraging, monitoring and optimizing the learning of pupils. Teachers would be honoured if they prove themselves to be true friends, philosophers and guides of the community they serve. The society also would appreciate if the teachers' response is positive and helpful for the total community. Commitment of the teachers to the local community should gradually extend to the whole society. Since the teachers are considered to be nation builders, it is extremely important for teacher education to develop this commitment in the teachers as well as teacher educators to help them contribute constructively and meaningfully for wholesome development of the society.

The teachers should be willing to understand the local community and participate in various activities related to the development of the school and community and also be able to internalise the value of their own day to day work in developing a rich human resource for the advancement of the individual learner, family, local community and the larger society. The teachers should understand and realise invaluable significance of their work for national development.

Commitment to the Profession

This commitment area involves two essential components namely; pride in one's being in the teaching profession and a strong desire for professional development. However, with the expansion of educational facilities in the country, many of the teachers join this profession not because of any kind of inner compulsion or love for the profession but due to situational constraints. In fact, after joining the profession they should fully understand that as long as they are there, they have to develop pride, knowing well that this is a noble profession charged with great responsibilities as the society hands over its children to this system for their wholesome education, development and proper socialisation. Imparting rudiments of the learning process is just one of many demands on the teachers. Educating children is indeed empowering them. This process needs total involvement.

During and even after school hours, a committed teacher's mind remains always occupied with thoughts of children, their growth, individually as well as collectively and improvement of their performance.

Committed teachers not only seek all round development of children put to their charge but also work hard for their own professional growth to contribute their best to the profession as teachers. They observe professional ethics befitting the nobility of the profession.

Commitment to Attaining Excellence for Professional Action

Professionally committed teachers' first love is their quest for knowledge and excellence, both on their quest for knowledge and excellence, both on their own part as well as on the part of their students. They are always keen to achieve the best through their performance as teachers in terms of acquisition and transmission of knowledge as also by their words as well as action. They try to attain excellence in the entire teaching-learning process through their constant quest for becoming better and better teachers. Naturally, teacher education must try to develop this first love among the teachers during their pre-service teacher preparation programme and should try to keep it up through in-service teacher education as well, in order to firmly establish this commitment as part of their personal and professional culture as teacher.

Commitment to Basic Values

Teachers' commitment to basic values is very important. The value system always acts as radar and shows to the human beings the way to follow, even though it differs not only from community to community but also from person to person. However, there are certain common values, other than those enshrined in the constitution, which need to be reflected in the teachers' feeling, willing and doing and indeed as manifestation of their behaviour as teachers. These include honesty, cooperation, love, truth, objectivity, regularity, punctuality, etc., which need to be reflected in teachers' feeling, willing and doing. Observance of these values by the teachers as a role model can create a great impact on the impressionable minds of the pupils as an integral part of their personality.

COMMITMENT IN TEACHING PROFESSION

Commitment is a state of mind, which positively affects the efficiency of teaching profession. It has also been studied as phenomena on mental attitude of the teachers, towards their profession, affected by other variables—particularly, the mobility. Backer has made systematic inductive study of imaginary committed teachers to identify some indicators of commitment, which constitute the index of commitment.

The index of commitment in teaching profession may be classified as:

(*a*) Positive Indicators

(*b*) Negative Indicators

(a) Positive Indicators: Some of the important positive indicators of teachers' commitment are:

1. Awareness of the duties of a teacher; 2. Academic competence and will to improve upon it; 3. Awareness of the latest methods of teaching i.e. professional competence and will to improve upon it; 4. Understanding of the child psychology; 5. Interest in the wholesome development of the personality of the students; 6. Patience to and sympathy with the students; 7. Tactfulness and resourcefulness; 8. Punctuality and regularity; 9. Sincerity; 10. An idea of the management of time in order to cover the syllabus and do justice to each topic; 11. Able to control the class and maintain discipline; 12. Commanding respect from the students; 13. Making efforts to keep in touch with the parents for the benefit of the students; 14. Helping in administrative work; 15. Helping in organizing co-curricular activities; 16. Job-satisfaction and feeling of pleasure in performing role as a teacher; 17. Will to continue in the teaching profession; 18. A dependable and willing worker; 19. A person with strong character.

The above positive indicators of commitment are the expression of those qualities of a teacher, the possession of which indicate professional commitment. Not only possession of certain qualities but expression of teacher's love for the children, the teaching subject, the institution and the profession as a whole are also positive indicators of commitment to the profession. Teaching profession does not imply teaching only, it also includes all the other things associated with teaching. Each of them shall be taken one by one.

The first concern of a committed teacher is the welfare and education of her students. Teacher is aware of his/her responsibility towards the wholesome development of the personality of students. He/she tries to inculcate self confidence, patriotism, critical judgement and creativity among her students. He/she plans his/her teaching according to the physical, mental limitation and the emotional make up of his/her students. He/she has an estimate of the level of receptivity of his/her students and their problems. Teacher has a good understanding of child psychology and applies for the benefit of the students. He/she deals with students with unlimited patience and sympathy.

Not only the students but the subject that he/she is teaching is also important to her. He/she likes the subjects and tries to keep abreast with the latest information about it. A good understanding of the subjects enables him/her to do justice with each topic of the syllabus. A committed teacher has a sense of proper distribution of time for each topic and he/she is able to produce good results.

A committed teacher is able to control the class and maintain proper discipline in the class. He/She commands respect from his/her students. Students obey him/her not because of the fear of punishment but because of their respect for him/her. He/she is judicial in giving reward/ punishment, praise and blame.

He/she makes constant efforts to improve his/her own professional competence. He/She is aware of the latest information about the subject and the methods of teaching it. He/she makes experiment of his/her own in order to find out the best method of teaching and imparting knowledge. She makes extra efforts to make her teaching effective and interesting.

A committed teacher also shows concern for the institution as a whole. Her concern over general neatness and cleanliness of the school building, its reputation, formulation of sound traditions etc., are all positive indicators of commitment to teaching profession. He/she takes interest in the proper organization of school activities, cultural programmes, sports, debates inter-school competitions, excursions and picnics etc.

He/she is aware of the social, political, national and international problems of the country. His/her awareness of the world situation helps her to impart education in reference to the national and international conditions of the times.

A committed teacher is also co-operative. He/she is able to establish good rapport with the students, staff, the principal and the parents. He/ she understands that their cooperation is in the interest of the students.

A committed teacher is a sincere worker. He/She performs his/her duties not for the sake of show or for fear of the boss. He/she is aware of his/her duties and responsibilities and discharges them without fear of supervision or control. He/she possesses strong character and works with determination. He/she has the qualities of punctuality and regularity.

Above all, a committed teacher derives satisfaction and pleasure from doing his/her job to the best of his/her capacity. He/she does not consider his/her job as a necessary burden. He/she gets a feeling of fulfillment and satisfaction by performing his/her duties as a teacher. He/she would not like to change his/her possession for the sake of petty gains and comforts. He/she is a willing worker and an asset to the school.

(b)Negative Indicators: 1. Refusal to take up more gainful job or occupation; 2. Sacrifice of one's own leisure time; 3. Sacrifice of money. 4. Minimization of one's own needs; 5. Neglect of one's own family; 6. Control over one's temper; 7. Sacrifice of one's own pleasure; 8.Less critical to others.

All these indicators help to measure the degree of commitment of teachers. Professional commitment does not only consist in what a teacher is willing to do for his/her profession. Self denial or not-doing of certain things also indicates commitment.

It is observed that often committed teachers sacrifice their time, energy and money for the sake of their profession. They deny themselves the leisure time in which they could take rest and relax. They spend more time with the students or for the sake of other school responsibilities by either coming earlier to the school or by staying in the school even after the school hours. Spending more time for the sake of professional responsibilities, taxes on their own leisure time and energy. If need be, they even work on Sunday and holidays. In discharging school responsibilities, often they have to spend their own money. They buy relevant books, magazines and teaching aids on their own expense, so that these things may prove useful for his/her students.

Often it is seen that his/her own children and family members suffer from lack of attention because of her commitment to her profession. Though sacrifices made by the family members of the committed teachers fall outside the scope of present study, it is apparent that a committed teacher heavily depends on the basic understanding and co-operation of her family members, that it is relevant and worth-mentioning over here. A committed teacher usually neglects her own comforts and needs, on the strength of the extra support of his/ her family members. Sometimes when this basic understanding, support and co-operation are missing, the task of a committed teacher becomes even more difficult. He/she has to struggle even harder to excel in his/her profession, as well as in keeping her family members happy. Task of a committed teacher is very demanding. She cannot altogether afford to neglect his/her family, nor it is needed every time. Often, the comforts of staying at home are sacrificed for the sake of professional demands. He/she does just enough so that he/she is not singled out for not doing certain things. Often some teachers do certain things just for the sake of face saving or when the principal or some other senior is watching. In contrast to these teachers, a committed teacher performs his/her duties for her own satisfaction and welfare of the students. Thus there is a difference in the quality of performance of a committed and a less committed teacher. She makes sacrifices, not because some body else has asked her to do that, but because doing his/her duties as a teacher to the maximum of his/her capacity gives him/her satisfaction and happiness.

A less committed teacher also performs his/her role as a teacher and does all the things that are required from a teacher, but she does not make extra efforts to excel in his/ her work.

The current accepted conceptualizations of teacher commitment can be directly linked back to the research done in the 1970's into organizational commitment by Kanter (1974) and Mowday, Steers and Porter (1979). Teachers are thought to have commitments to the social context in which they work; Kanter describes it as the 'Social System'. Teacher commitment is not one dimensional but has many layers and dimensions (Day, 2000, 2004; Nias, 1981, 1996; Tyree, 1996). Individual teacher's commitment in their professional practice means commitment to (*a*) the school or organization (Graham,1996; Huber, 1999; Louis, 1998; Tsui & Cheng, 1999), (*b*) students (Bilken, 1995; Nias,1981; Tyree, 1996; Yong, 1999), (*c*) Career continuance (Nias, 1981; Tyree, 1996; Wood, 1981; Yong, 1999), (*d*) Professional knowledge base (Nias, 1981; Tyree, 1996), (*e*) the teaching profession (Day, 2000, 2004; Tyree, 1996).

COMMITMENT AND CONTRIBUTING FACTORS

Here, professional commitment means teachers commitment to their job as teachers. It corresponds to commitment to work put forward by Fink (1992), which is related to organization, co-worker and work.

As teaching profession comprises a considerable number of members, so it is a large organization. Based on an analogy to organizational commitment defined by Mowday and McDade (1979), professional commitment is characterized by the following factors:

- A strong belief in and acceptance of the profession's goals and values.
- A willingness to exert considerable effort on behalf of the profession.
- A strong desire to maintain membership in the profession.

Numerous studies have suggested that employees' job attitudes and commitment can affect their performance (Camann et al.1983; Oldham and Hickman, 1981). For personal factors, they include locus of control (Cheng, 1990), age, tenure, gender and education level (Fink, 1992). Non-demographic individual difference variables include central life interest (Dubin et al. 1975), desire for greater job responsibility, expectations about goal achievements and personal need (Steers, 1977).

Other factors such as lateness, absenteeism, tardiness and turnover are the manifestations of commitment as reflected in most literature.

Cole (1979) and Sekaran (1989) have stated in their studies that employees 'stay back' are also a manifestation of commitment and can be used as a predictor of commitment level.

James W. Kushman in his study focussed on two types of teacher workplace commitment: organizational commitment and commitment to student learning. Organizational commitment means a sense of teacher loyalty to the school workplace and identification with its values and goals (Mowday, Porter & Steers, 1982). Conceptually, this type of commitment is related to building staff unity of purpose and an agreed on school mission. Commitment to student learning reflects teacher dedication to helping students learn, regardless of their academic difficulties or social background. Conceptually, this type of commitment speaks to increasing students' engagement in learning and academic achievement, particularly for students who are academically at risk. Each type of commitment is briefly reviewed and the rationale is given in his study by two particular commitment variables. In his study, he describes organizational commitment refers to degree that an individual internalizes organizational values and goals a sense of loyalty to the workplace. This type of commitment reflects an alignment between individual and organizational needs and values, thereby resulting in a strong unity of purpose among workers and work groups. Katz and Kahn (1978) discussed organizational commitment as an intrinsic motivation factor where the internalization of organizational values represents a more powerful source of employee motivation than compliance or extrinsic rewards. Commitment does not depend on coercive control or a continual stream of rewards but is self-sustaining once it is achieved.

Etzioni (1961) made an important conceptual distinction between two types of commitment: 'Calculative' commitment and 'moral' commitment. Calculative commitment embodies cognitive decision process of weighing alternatives and costs/benefits in individual investments in an organization (e.g., salary, pension and status) that figure in considerations to stay or leave. Moral commitment, on the other hand, is a distinct attitudinal component of the individual internalizing organizational values provides an important perspective on employee motivation, particularly in organizations like schools where normative and symbolic control take precedence over material incentives and rewards (Meyer & Rowan, 1978; Weick, 1976; Weiner, 1982).

Much of the research on organizational commitment has used a three-part definition of the construct developed by Porter and his colleagues (Mowday et al., 1982; Mowday, Steers & Porter, 1979; Porter, Steers, Mowday, & Boulian, 1974). These components are (*a*) the willingness of the individual to exert effort on behalf of the organization, (*b*) a desire to stay with the organization and (*c*) acceptance of its major values and goals. The first component is almost synonymous with the idea of work motivation (Campbell & Pritchard, 1977) and clearly places commitment within the motivational domain. The second component describes loyalty and like the first, hints of behavioral intentions rather than attitudes per se. Finally, the third component describes an alignment between individual and organizational values and goals that allows the organization to achieve its ends.

The research on organizational commitment has covered a range of occupations and job levels in both public and private organizations. Human service and public service workers, such as nurses, mental health workers, and federal employees, have received particular attention because these are occupations bearing some resemblance to the occupation of school teacher. A study by Hrebiniak and Aluto (1972) compared the organizational commitment of elementary and high school teachers to nurses and found identical levels of commitment and no moderating effects of occupation on relationships between commitment and antecedent variables. Hence, even though this body of research does not focus heavily on school teachers, it does have some relevance to the extent that findings generalize across similar occupational types. The research has tended to be co-relational, focusing on relationships between organizational commitment and hypothesized antecedents and outcomes.

Employee background characteristics and more alterable job and organizational characteristics have been found to be predictive of organizational commitment (Giffen & Bateman, 1986). Older workers tend to have higher levels of organizational commitment compared to younger ones, whereas education shows an inverse relationship with more educated workers reporting lower levels of commitment (Angle & Perry, 1981; Fukami & Larson, 1984; Hrebinaik, 1974; Hrebiniak & Aluto, 1972, on school teachers; Koch & Steers, 1978; Morris & Sherman, 1981; Stevens, Beyers, & Trice, 1978). Regarding job characteristics, employees report high levels of organizational commitment when their work includes a high degree of autonomy, task identity, and participation in decision making (Fukami & Larson, 1984; Morris & Steers, 1980; Rhodes & Steers, 1981; Steers, 1977; Stevens et al., 1978), and low levels of commitment when job produces role conflict, role ambiguity, or stress (Fukami & Larson, 1984; Hrebinaik & Aluto, 1972, on school teachers; Morris & Sherman, 1981; Steers, 1977; Stevens et al., 1978). Employees' leaving the organization (turnover) is the major behavioural outcome consistently associated with low levels of organizational commitment, and there is also evidence that low commitment is linked to high absenteeism (Angle & Perry, 1981; Koch & Steers, 1978; Porter, Crampon & Smith, 1976; Porter et al., 1974; Steers, 1977). The evidence suggests that organizational commitment is a function of both the worker and the workplace and that low commitment can have costly negative effects on organizational performance in the forms of high turnover and absenteeism.

Hoy and Ferguson (1985), using a sample of high schools found strong positive relationships between teacher organizational commitment and staff cohesiveness and attitudes towards innovation. These results suggest that high commitment may play a role in shaping school norms of collegiality and continuous improvement that are part of the formula for academically effective inner-city schools (Little, 1982; Rosenholtz, 1985). Although Hoy and Ferguson found no statistical relationship between teacher organization commitment and student academic achievement, they did find a relationship between commitment and staff and expert ratings of organizational effectiveness. Rosenholtz (1989) looked at predictors of teacher workplace commitment, defined as satisfaction with teaching in the current school and a desire to remain there, in 78 rural and urban schools and found a cluster of important predictor variables that reflected the degree of 'professional fulfillment' that teachers experience in their everyday work. Rosenholtz also found some support for a relationship between teacher commitment and student achievement, but here the results were weak and inconclusive. Although both studies are illuminating, the used weak measures of student achievement, precluding a good test of the important linkage between teacher commitment and student achievement. So, from the discussion, it is concluded that organizational commitment represents a powerful motivational force in schools given that other motivational means, such as extrinsic rewards or bureaucratic rules, are not very feasible.

Commitment to student learning was conceptualized as consisting of three interrelated components: a sense of teacher efficacy, the expectation that students will learn, and the willingness to put forth the effort required for student learning to occur, particularly for low achieving students. The first two components mirror the effective schools notion that 'all students can learn,' and the third includes the teacher effort required to make learning happen. The theoretical underpinnings for this concept are (*a*) the works of Ashton and Webb (1986) on teacher efficacy and (*b*) the effective schools research dealing with teacher expectations for student success. Ashton and Webb (1986) defined teacher efficacy as the belief that teaching can lead to student learning even when obstacles to learning are present, such as low student ability or a disadvantaged background. In their ethnographic study of a 'progressive' middle school, Ashton and Webb found that a high sense of efficacy was associated with teacher attitudes and behaviors that are likely to result in high student achievement. These attitudes/behaviors included less blaming of students for failure, feeling more responsible for student self development, and a movement away from a single-method teaching approach to situation-specific teaching where the objective was student understanding rather than completing prescribed lessons. In a more systematic analysis at the classroom level (n=45 high school classrooms), Ashton and Webb found that teacher efficacy made a substantial contribution to predicting student math and language achievement gains but not reading. They postulated that teacher efficacy positively affects student achievement, a relationship mediated by (*a*) a more personalized teaching style, (*b*) a student sense of efficacy, and (*c*) student behaviors reflecting more enthusiasm and initiation of student-teacher contacts.

A high teacher expectation for student learning is one of Edmonds's (1979) five factors for academically effective schools. The work of Brooker, Beady, Flood, Schweitzer, and Wisenbaker (1979) lends further support to the importance of teacher expectations as well as teacher commitment. The Brooker et al. study of Michigan elementary schools found that high teacher expectations for student learning and a strong teacher commitment to improve helped explain school wide achievement after controlling for student background characteristics. Research on teacher expectations has a longer history, of course, beginning with the 'Pygmalion in the classroom' studies in the 1960s and continuing with studies of how ability grouping can influence teacher expectations and subsequent teaching behavior (Brophy & Good, 1974; Good & Brophy, 1984; Green, 1987). These studies have shown that both positive and negative teacher expectations can influence teacher instructional behaviors in predictable ways.

Commitment to student learning is grounded in the ideas of high teacher efficacy and high expectations, while adding a third supporting dimension of teacher willingness to exert effort on behalf of low-achieving students. The efficacy and expectations research provide support for a linkage between commitment to student learning and student achievement, although the causal direction of this relationship is open to question.

Gupta and Pande (1999) studied commitment level of polytechnic teachers, and strategies to enhance it. They found the polytechnic teachers have indicated a high level of commitment in activities related to student counselling, teaching, co-curricular and extra curricular activities and innovation in instruction. Medium level of commitment in student assessment and evaluation, curriculum development, revenue generation and developing resource material, continuing education, research and development and community service. So willingness, role status, information sharing, freedom, values and beliefs, participation, training and development, problem solving, job-satisfaction, innovativeness, leadership, rewards, employee's relation, Involvement in profession, supervision, excellence, organizational pride, work practices, performance and team work were the factors in order of priority contributing positively to the organizational commitment.

It is obvious from above stated facts that commitment is the consistency in the lines of behaviour to an organization or occupation. Professional commitment of teachers contributes to their efficiency, quality of teaching and achievement of goals of the school. From some studies it is clear that job-satisfaction, role status, employer's relation, teamwork, organizational pride, etc are the factors contributing to organizational commitment. Personal factors like age, locus of control, gender, educational level and personal needs also affect professional commitment.

STUDIES RELATED TO OCCUPATIONAL STRESS, JOB-SATISFACTION AND PROFESSIONAL COMMITMENT

Bhatt (1997) studied "Job-stress, job involvement and job-satisfaction of teachers: A correlation study." He found that the teacher's job stress was significantly, negatively associated with their job involvement and job satisfaction; whereas job involvement was highly significantly, positively correlated with the teacher's job satisfaction. Four factors of job stress were significantly negatively correlated with their overall job satisfaction. There existed a significant, negative partial correlation with their overall teacher's job stress and their job involvement but there was a negative, insignificant, partial correlation between the job stress and job satisfaction. The teacher's job involvement was significantly, positively and partially correlated with their satisfaction.

Chhokar (1995) assessed the role and organizational correlates of job-satisfaction, job involvement, organizational commitment, and psychological strain among bank employees. Role ambiguity and role conflict were low; role overload, participation in decision-making, hierarchy of authority and the subset of organizational values representing consideration of employees were moderate; and formalization and the sub-set of organizational value representing contribution to the organization were fairly high. While psychological strain was observed to be fairly low, job satisfaction, job-involvement, and organizational commitment were higher. The subset organizational values representing consideration for employed was the only variable that consistently predicted all four criterion variables; they contributed to increased job-satisfaction, job involvement, organizational commitment, and low psychological strain. Role ambiguity was significantly related to increased psychological strain and reduced job satisfaction and organizational commitment. Mishra and Srivastava (2000) reported that role ambiguity moderated the relationship between affective commitment and job satisfaction among doctors.

There are several studies in the area of job-satisfaction, involvement and commitment. A finding, replicated more than once in different contexts, is the overlapping relationship between job-involvement, satisfaction, and commitment. It is clear that these concepts are not mutually exclusive.

Commitment to the organization and job-involvement, were above average to high in most situations. Like job-involvement and satisfaction, role clarity, consideration, age, and nature of task also influenced commitment. In addition, commitment was related to availability of slack perception of fairness, and presence of threat, and frustration. Value congruence was not related to commitment, but was related to intentions that led to commitment. Different predictors were observed for men, women and skilled workers.

The samples used in studies of job-involvement, satisfaction, and commitment are diverse in nature consisting of bankers, teachers, doctors, and industrial workers. The findings are varied, but a consistent finding is the influence of nature of work and overall organizational climate in predicting the relationship with work. Only two studies have examined the opposite of commitment or involvement that is alienation and perception of deprivation.

Much work has been done on job involvement, organizational commitment, and job satisfaction. Singh and Nath (1991) explored the effects of organizational role stress, organizational climate and locus of control on the job involvement of bank employees. Employees high on role stress exhibited lower job involvement than those low on role stress.

R.A Joshi (1993) not only noted that women were less committed to their organization than men but also found evidence of different determinants of commitment. Factors such as satisfaction with firm, number of dependants and family income determined organizational commitment in the case of women. For men, the determinants of commitment were satisfaction with work.

The experience of stress on the job was negatively correlated with job satisfaction and organizational commitment. The effects of six lifestyles stressors-performance, threat, boredom, frustration, bereavement, and physical conditions on organizational commitment effectiveness across job levels were studied by U.N. Biswas (1998). Performance, threat and frustration were significant predictors of organizational commitment. However, none of the stressors significantly predicted job involvement.

Managers obtained significantly higher scores on organizational commitment and job involvement than supervisors and workers. Also, workers reported significantly higher performance stress than managers and supervisors. Organizational commitment, job involvement, and perceived organizational effectiveness were positively correlated with each other.

Higher job satisfaction is related to lower occupational stress and vice versa (Borg et al. 1991; Burke & Greenglass, 1994; Davis & Wilson, 2000; Day Bedian & Conte, 1998; Kyriacou & Sutcliffe, 1979; Laughlin, 1984; Manthei & Gilmore, 1996; Mc Cormick, 1997b). Studies that have examined the dimensions of job satisfaction and stress variables and have provided a more through picture of how job stress and satisfaction are related; various analyses have shown that stress factors such as role ambiguity, role conflict and role overload have different strength of relationships are generally negative (Currivan, 2000; Ray & Miller, 1991; Smith & Bourke, 1992; Starnmen & Miller, 1992). Currivan (2000) reported that role ambiguity was more strongly related to job satisfaction than role conflict. Role ambiguity and role conflict had relationship of various strength with extrinsic and intrinsic job satisfaction (Summers, Decotis & DeNisi, 1995). A direction of casuality cannot be specified for job satisfaction and occupational stress. They influence one another. Otto (1986) reported that occupational stress was highest among the most dissatisfied teachers and lowest among the satisfied. Otto also cautioned that satisfied teachers were not without stress and this suggests that the relationship between stress and satisfaction is more complex. Bonnie S. Billingsley and Lawrence H. Cross in their study "Predictors of Commitment, job satisfaction and intent to stay in teaching: A comparision of general and specific educators" found that work related variables such as leadership support, role conflict, role ambiguity are better predictors of commitment and job satisfaction than demographic variables. More experienced and highly educated often reported just as much stress and deterioration of job commitment as experienced and less educated teachers (George, et al., 1995; Pullis, 1992). Singh and Billingsley (1996) reported a moderate positive correlation for experience and intent to remain in the profession among teachers of emotional and behaviour disorder students, high levels of education did not predict intent to stay in the field. Excessive paper work and lack of administrative support were consistently cited as sources of stress, dissatisfaction and attrition, while positive working environment were often indications of satisfied teachers of emotion and behaviour disorder students (George et al., 1995; Lawrenson & Mc Kinnon, 1982; Mc Manus & Kauffman, 1991; Pullis, 1992; Singh & Billingsley, 1996)

In a study of Australian teachers, Mc Cormick (1997b) reported that job satisfaction was more strongly associated with stress from external forces (Such as system expectations and govt. policies) than stress arising from personal issues (such as perceived suitability to teaching). On the otherhand, teachers reporting higher job satisfaction were more likely to identify stress arising from personal issues as sources of stress. Corrigan, Holmes and Luchins (1995) reported that satisfaction with collegial support was associated with diminished burnout. In another study of teachers, Smith and Bourke (1992) reported that satisfaction with school administration was associated with reduced stress arising from lack of rewards and recognition while satisfaction with work condition was related to diminished stress from time pressure.

From the above studies it is clear that job-stress was negatively related with job-involvement and job-satisfaction whereas job-involvement was highly positively correlated with the teachers' job-satisfaction. Satisfaction with organization, number of dependants and family income determined organizational commitment. There is overlapping relationship between job-involvement, job-satisfaction and professional commitment.

2

Review of Related Literature

Review of related literature plays a vital role in research. It acts as a guide, not only with regard to the work done in the field, but also to perceive the gaps and lacunas in the concerned field of research. It helps in understanding the potentialities of the problem in hand and enables the investigator to formulate hypotheses regarding possible solutions of the problem. Review focuses an in-depth insight in to the research project. It directs the investigator to move in a perfect path to achieve the desired outcome from the research work.

Here, it was not possible for the investigator to get access to the entire published and unpublished research in the field but still an attempt has been made to study the literature concerning investigation in the hand. The investigator has divided the work in the following sequence:

1. Studies on occupational stress;
2. Studies on job-satisfaction;
3. Studies on professional commitment.

Studies Related to Occupational Stress

Singh and others (1998) studied job stress among secondary school teachers in relation to management, sex and marital status. The results reveal that the main effects of the management of the schools-private or government were significant. Teachers of private schools had higher level of job stress than the teachers of Navodaya schools. A level of job stress was higher in both male and female private school teachers than the teachers of Navodaya schools. Both married and unmarried teachers of private schools had higher job stress as compared to the teachers of Navodaya schools. Both male and female teachers from privately managed institution had higher job stress. The interactive effect of teachers' marital status, management and sex did not contribute anything to the teachers' job stress.

Upadhayay and others (2001) studied occupational stress among college and school teachers. The results show that the higher secondary school teachers (HSST) showed significantly higher level of stress than the college teachers on the factors related to role overload, role ambiguity and role conflict fact that different expectation from their employees. Poor relationship with the peer group is always a cause of stress to anyone. College teachers and HSSTs differed significantly on this factor. The desire to get closer with the head of the institution for the personal benefits and show envy to the advancement of their colleagues could be the potent cause for the college teachers. The college teachers get more time to look after their personal works, have enough time, enjoy higher salary and associated benefits and have higher career expectations etc than the HSSTs.

Choudhary (2001) studied teacher's burnout in relation to occupational stress, mental health problems and socio-economic status a factor analytical study. The findings of the study are as follows (1) the main effects of occupational stress; mental health and socio-economic status on burnout were found to be insignificant. (2) The main effects of occupational stress, mental health and socio-economic status on the different dimensions of burnout were found to be significant. Occupational stress revealed significant effect on depersonalization. (3) F-ratio for the first order interaction between occupational stress and mental health on burn out came out to be significant. (*a*) Occupational stress and socio-economic status showed interactional effect on personal accomplishment. (4) The main effects of occupational stress, marital status and age group on burnout were found to be insignificant. (5) The main effects of occupational stress, teaching experience and educational qualification on burn-out were found to be insignificant. (6) The triple interaction between occupational stress, teaching experience and educational qualification on personal accomplishment of primary teachers was found to be in significant. (7) The main effects of occupational stress, sex and residence of teachers on their burn out were found to be insignificant. (8) The main effect of sex and residence on different dimensions was found to be insignificant. (9) The first order interaction between occupational stress, sex and residence on burnout and its three dimensions were found to be insignificant. The second order interaction on depersonalization was found to be significant.

Kirk and others (2002) studied job stress and dissatisfaction comparing male and female medical practitioners and auxiliary personnel. The results indicate that doctors have higher stress scores but higher job satisfaction than auxiliary personnel, that stress among doctors is positively correlated with work hours that stress in auxiliary personnel is positively correlated with age, gender and work hours but negatively correlated with job-satisfaction. The results also show that job- satisfaction is associated with age for doctors and auxiliary personnel and with marital status for auxiliary personnel that distance to work is predictive of work attitude for auxiliary personnel that female doctors perceive higher work stress than male doctors and female auxiliary personnel perceive lower work stress than male auxiliary.

Gellis and other (2002) studied coping with occupational stress in healthcare: A comparison of social workers and nurses The result indicate that social workers and nurses differed significantly on measures of perceived job stress, job satisfaction and the use of three coping methods. Separate multiple regressions were completed for social workers and nurses to examine the relative influence of job stress and coping on job-satisfaction. For both groups, perceived job stress was the greatest contributor to job satisfaction.

Michalidis and others (2002) studied occupational stress as it relates to higher education, individuals and organizations work. Preliminary findings showed that occupational stress has a negative impact on the degree of satisfaction with their achievement, value and growth, being strongest with faculty and coordinators (dissatisfaction with career opportunities, personal growth, and skill utilization). Another significant outcome was the dissatisfaction of faculty with the organizational design structure and processes (communication, change. implementation, motivation, supervisor style, participation in decision marking). All possess individual characteristics of the type A scale they all considered major sources of pressure in their jobs to be their relationship with others, homework interface, their need to achieve personal and corporate success. Occupational stress has affected their state of health.

Hutri and others (2002) studied the role of stress and negative emotions in an occupational crisis. The results showed that occupational crisis was a function of work overload, interpersonal problems and frustration at work; organizational changes, a threat of job less, and/ or family worries. In addition, occupational crisis were typically experienced by women and were characterized more by trait anxiety suppressed anger and depressive symptoms than by overtly expressed anger or state anxiety of the three female employee groups who were most vulnerable to the crisis, the groups which had suffered from interpersonal problems and frustration at work displayed the most indices of the crisis.

Teo, Claire and others (2002) studied the role of human resource practices in reading occupational stress and strain. Results indicate that human resource (HR) practices did not reduce the sources of stress (role overload and responsibility) within the work place However there was a direct negative relationship between HR practices and interpersonal strain. In particular, family friendly practices, job training and SMI (stress interventions) reduced interpersonal strain. An examination of vocational SMIs and job training, in addition, organizational commitment mediated the relationship between HR practices and vocational strain. It was concluded that HR practices might be effective as part of a Symptom-directed approach to stress intervention and that further replication of these results in both Asia and western samples is required.

Hogan and others (2002) studied stressors and stress reactions among University personnel. The principal results showed that job and non-work stress correlated positively with behavioural, cognitive and physiological reactions to stress as well as with negative emotionality. Job and non-work stress correlated meaningfully with medical symptoms, non-work stress also correlated at a useful level with reported medical utilization. Social support did not generally modulate reports of stress or reactions to stress. It was also found that support staff reported higher levels of non-work stress and lower levels of work stress but that measures of job stress did not differentiate administrative and instructional personnel. Younger staff reported higher levels of job and non-work stress and females reported higher level of non-work stress irrespective of job category.

Differences were found between reported occupational stress among public and private sector public relations officers. Higher stress was reported by public sector public relations officers (Misra, 1997). Similarly, bankers of non-nationalised banks reported higher stress levels as compared to those of nationalized banks (Aminabhavi & Triveni, 2000). Differences were found in role related stress experienced by male verses female school teachers working in general schools as compared to no gender based differences in teachers working in special schools. Teachers and professors scored high on emotional exhaustion intensity, emotional exhaustion frequency and depersonalization frequency.

In comparison of role stress experienced by officers, bankers and school teachers it was found that teachers experienced least role stress (Pareek & Mehta, 19997). Sultana (1995) noted significant differences between both professional male and female teachers on the dimensions of inter role distance, role stagnation, role erosion, role-overload and role ambiguity. Mishra (1996) reported that female teachers experienced greater role related stress, inter personal stress and work overload as compared to their male colleagues.

Gynaecologists and Paediatricians were more stressed emotionally exhausted and reported higher feelings of depersonalization as compared to surgeons and medicine specialists (Jagdish & Reddy, 2000). Rani Lakshmi and Mishra (2001) in a study of doctors and nurses, observed that profession had a significant effect on the experience of several facets of occupational role stress, namely, role expectation effect, role erosion, role overload, role isolation, personal inadequacy, self-role distance, role ambiguity and role inadequacy.

All categories of aviation personnel, cabinet attendants, engineers and pilots experienced higher stress levels than railway and roadway personnel (Barnes, 1992a). Majority of the scientists reported moderate to low stress (Savita & Asnani, 1998). A moderate level of stress was observed among women doctors, teachers, bank officers and bureaucrats (Gaur & Dhiman, 2000). Executives were found more stressed than physicians, especially in the area of role insufficiency (Ghosh, 2000).University teachers experienced less stressed than bank managers (Barkat & Parveen, 1999). Employees of administrative organizations reported greater stress than working in financial organization at the same level in the hierarchy (Sahoo, Mohanty & Bhakat, 1995). Nurses perceived more work stress than lecturers but did not express more personal strain (Orpen, 1996).

Tyagi and Sen (2000) found that female managers were more stressed than male managers and supervisors were more stressed than executives irrespective of gender. Male engineers experienced more stress than female engineers (Deosthalee, 2000). Chattopadhyay and Dasgupta (1999) did not find any significant differences in the perceived role stress among single and married female executives. The newspaper industry was higher than among non-video display terminal users (A. Singh, 1993). Similarly, it was also observed that video display terminal users were more stressed, anxious and fatigued than non-users (Arora, 1994). Employees of nationalized banks reported lesser burnout but higher emotional exhaustion than those of scheduled banks (Tewari, 1995).

Cross-cultural Comparison of Perception of Stress

In a comparison of personal and professional stressors experienced by Indian and American executives working in banks, textile mills, pharmaceutical, engineering, petrochemical and electrical industries it was found that professional stressors were similar in both countries. However, personal stressors were different in both countries and Indian executives experienced more personal stressors (Batlivala, 1990).

Similarly, a comparison of Indian and American female clerical employees revealed that the source of stress among American clerks was lack of control/ autonomy whereas among Indians it was lack of structure and clarity of task (Narayanan, Menon & Spector, 1999).

Stress and Personality

S.C. Pandey (1998) studied the relationship between personality dimensions and organizational role stress in a public sector organizational role stress in a public sector organization. There were no differences in the role stress of middle level managers, lower level managers and supervisors. The psychoticism-reality and neuroticism stability dimensions of personality were positively related to subjects' perceived organizational role stress (ORS). The Extroversion-Introversion dimension was negatively related to role stress.

Ahmad, James and Ahmad (1991) examined the relationship between ORS and job satisfaction and personality dimensions of neuroticism-stability and extroversion and introversion among middle level managers. Results indicated that ORS was significantly but negatively correlated with all four factors of job satisfaction (nature of job, management, personal adjustment and social relation). The neuroticism-stability dimension of personality was significantly and positively related to six dimensions of ORS. Only one dimension of ORS, that is, role expectation conflict had a significantly negative relationship with extroversion-introversion.

Sharma, Sood and Speilberger (1998) investigated the correlation between occupation and occupational stress, anxiety, anger and Type A behaviour among registered nurses (age 22-48 years) working in four state administered hospitals of Himachal Pradesh. Those with Type A behaviours were highly stressed, more likely to repress anger and manifested higher trait anxiety. Type A subjects reported greater affective discomfort than their Type B counterparts.

Another study of male bankers reported that external locus of control was correlated with role related stress in their role expectations, role overload and role ambiguity facets (Malik & Sabharwal, 1999). Role ambiguity was negatively correlated with external locus of control among university teachers (Joshi & Singhvi, 1997)

Machiavellianism was not found to be correlated with stress among teachers (Joshi & Singhvi, 2000). The level of assertiveness of police officers was not related to the level of stress faced by them (Misra, 1997). Creativity was positively correlated with adaptation and stress among 55 middle level managers (Goklaney, 1993). No significant correlation was evidenced between problem solving style and occupational styles in a study of 150 executives of a government organization (Panchanatham, Rajendran & Karuppiah, 1993).

Stress was found to be influenced by age, general ability, and personality factors among 200 male executives (Reddy & Ramamurti, 1991). Age was positively correlated with stress among 80 executives (Beena & Poduval, 1991). Role related stress did not differ with age among bankers (Chaudhary, 1990). However, stress levels were higher in the case of younger female teachers (Ushashree & Jamuna, 1990). There was a positive but non-significant relationship between age and role related stress among railway personnel (Pandey, 1997b). Age had no significant impact on stress levels among male and female engineers (Deosthalee, 2000).

Male executives with masculine sex role orientation were higher on role stress as compared to female executives with androgynous sex role orientation (Aditya & Sen, 1993). Education was negatively correlated with stress experienced by engineers (Deosthalee, 2000).

Role Stress Among Working Women

Some studies have attempted to trace the particular stressors dominant among working women. Tharakan (1992) found that professional working women experienced greater work related stress than non-professional working women. Also, occupational stress and job satisfaction were significantly correlated with the professional qualification of women. Sekhar (1996) found that the type of hospital differentially affected the experience of job stress and burnout among female nurses. The number of patients that were assigned also significantly affected the nurses' helplessness, depersonalization experiences and personal accomplishment. Daga (1997) found that quality of life was correlated negatively but significantly with social family role stress among female clerks, doctors and teachers. Further, quality of life was associated positively and significantly with social support among clerks and teachers.

Kumar and Murty (1998) observed that the most frequently experienced stressors among women managers were office politics, followed by conflict between work and home, commuting to the workplace, lack of opportunity and challenge at the workplace and problems related to child care. The major strains experienced by women managers were anxiety, tension and fatigue, lack of concentration, irritation and physical health problems. Further, the most frequently used coping strategies were talking with spouse/ friends/parents/supervisors/colleagues about the problem, followed by efforts to increase knowledge/ information, physical withdrawal from the situation for a while, pursuing socio-cultural religious activities and doing physical exercise/ yoga/ meditation. Gaur and

Dhawan (2000) noted that women professionals used active coping stance, planfulness and initiative as adaptive patterns in the workplace. Mathur and Singhvi (1997) examined the relationship between organizational role stress and organizational ethos among 400 women in four professions, viz., doctors, school teachers, college teachers and bank employees. All the women were high on proaction and openness dimensions. Doctors, college teachers and bank employees were also high on collaboration and experimentation. In the case of all the women, inter role distance and role overload were positively associated with confrontation and experimentation dimensions. Role stagnation was correlated significantly with all the dimensions of organizational ethos. Job related strain was positively related to strenuous working conditions, role overload and role conflict among junior management officers (Chand & Sethi, 1997). The length of tenure among teachers was positively correlated with stress (Akhtar & [illegible]adra, 1990)

Professionals in various fields who perceived higher social support were less affected by the stress experienced at the workplace (Baerjee & Gupta, 199[illegible]; Singh & Srivastava, 1996). The perception of social support was found to reduce stress among teachers (Sud & Malik, 1999).

Role related stress was negatively correlated with quality of work life and sociopolitical alienation at the workplace in general (Ahmad & Mehta, 199[illegible]) among middle level managers/ supervisors of both private and public sector organizations. Overall role related stress was correlated positively with despair, normlessness and meaninglessness-al variants of alienation (Sehgal, 1997). Perceived role stress was negatively associated with trust and positively associated with distrust among executives working in private and public sector organizations (Dwivedi, 1997).

Alienation and organizational frustration was high in private sector managers as compared to public sector managers (Mishra, Bhardwaj & Mishra, 19[illegible]). The opposite trend was observed by Mohan and Chauhan (1999) for middle level managers. The study reported that public sector managers were more stressed than private sector employees and they perceived the work culture as unsupportive.

Stress and its Correlation with Job Involvement and Job Commitment

Job stress was negatively correlated with job involvement among 50 middle level hotel managers (Ahmad & Khanna, 1992), among executives working in a refinery (Jagdish & Singh, 1997), among middle level managers working in various departments (Singh & Singh, 1997). Perceived stress was found to be also negatively correlated with job satisfaction among bankers (Chaudhary, 19[illegible]0).

Kaur (2002) studied occupational stress among elementary school teachers in relation to role conflict, job satisfaction and biographic variables. The findings show that: (1) experience, income, qualification & marital status indicated differences in occupational stress scores independently as main effects; (2) The joint influence of first order interaction between income and school indicated significant differences in occupational stress scores; (3) Experience, income, qualifications and marital status, created differences in job satisfaction scores independently as main effects; (4) The joint influence of first order and second order interaction of (*i*) sex and experience (*ii*) income and school (*iii*) qualification, Marital status and locality (2nd order) in occupational stress; (5) Male and female teachers differed significantly in occupational stress; (6) The teachers belonging to different levels of job-satisfaction revealed significant differences in occupational stress; (7) No differences were found in occupational stress of elementary school teachers under the joint influence of different levels of sex and job satisfaction; (8) There were no difference in occupational stress scores, job satisfaction and role conflict among elementary school teachers when tested independently under the influence of different levels of religion.

Fair brother and others (2003) studied workplace dimensions, stress and job-satisfaction. They indicated strong connections between dimensions of the workplace stress and job-satisfaction. The result indicated that a general model of stress is unhelpful in identifying the predictors of stress and job-satisfaction in specific job contexts. Instead the authors recommended identifying salient workplace dimensions rather than a broad-brush approach when seeking workplace association with stress.

To conclude, the findings of these studies show that the factors of occupational stress are role overload, role conflict, role ambiguity, poor peer relationship, under participation, powerlessness etc. Occupational stress has negative impact on job-satisfaction, values, growth as well as on health.

STUDIES RELATED TO JOB SATISFACTION

Adval et al. (1961) investigated into the possible causes of failure in high school examinations. They found a number of causes for student failure in the examination. One of the findings was that low academic achievement was the consequence of unsatisfactory service conditions and inefficiency of teachers as reported by the principals of the schools.

Indiresan (1973) did a multivariate analysis of factors affecting job satisfaction of engineering teachers and investigated the relationship between certain individuals and situational variables and job satisfaction and concluded that none of the background variables i.e age, educational experience, etc. seemed to be related to job satisfaction. Job satisfaction and research output were found to be associated positively and none of the personality variables studied, except the job involvement was found to be related with job satisfaction.

Marr and Mathur (1973) studied the job satisfaction of teacher educators with respect to different work values. It was found that the largest teacher educators were satisfied with the fact that they found their work interesting. The author also pointed out that "it is necessary to create conditions which will enable teacher educators to use their minds, have the opportunity to accomplish some thing and to do work they consider useful and creative, as well as to have satisfying human relationship in their work."

Lavingia (1974) made an attempt to study job satisfaction among primary and secondary school teachers and found that female teachers were more satisfied than male teachers, young teachers were more satisfied than old teachers, whereas efficient performance of a job was positively related with the degree of satisfaction. There did not seem to be any relationship between academic qualification and job satisfaction among secondary school teachers but among primary teachers better qualified teachers were less satisfied, while the amount of satisfaction decreased with advance in age and dissatisfaction was highest in the age group of 40-44 years for secondary teachers and 35-39 years for primary teachers.

Singh (1974) measured teachers' values and studied their relationship with their attitudes and job satisfaction and found that teachers were moderately satisfied with all factors but female teachers were more satisfied than male teachers. Teachers' age, training, level of education, teaching experience was not related with their job satisfaction significantly.

Arora (1976) studied the difference between effective and ineffective teachers and found that differentiating characteristics of job satisfaction were general satisfaction as well as the degree of satisfaction with work and causes of satisfaction. He further stated teachers did not differ in terms of the length of teaching experience, satisfaction with the allotment of teaching subjects, textbooks and the mode of transport used for travelling to school.

Kotte (1978) made an investigation to identify the factors that are responsible for primary school teacher's satisfaction and dissatisfaction and reported that teachers' achievement, recognition and work itself were factors of job satisfaction and the causes of job dissatisfactions were unfair policy and administration, working conditions, salary and interpersonal relationship among the teachers.

Goyal (1980) tried to find out relationship among attitudes, job satisfaction, adjustment and professional interest of teacher educators and found that a large majority of the teacher educators were favourably inclined towards their profession and satisfaction in the job. The attitude and satisfaction of teacher educators did not differ significantly, while attitude, job satisfaction and occupational adjustment among teacher educators were associated with one another. Job satisfaction could be predicted by attitude and occupational adjustment but not by other variables.

Ahmad (1986) examined the determinations of job involvement among college teachers and found that job involvement was positively correlated with job satisfaction of college teachers. Some values, such as ability utilization, achievement and economic gains were negatively co-related with job satisfaction whereas social relations, prestige and autonomy were positively associated with job satisfaction of college teachers. Some job attributes, such as variety, autonomy, interaction and feedback contributed to job satisfaction.

Balwinder Kaur (1986) examined job satisfaction of home science school and college teachers and its relationship with personal, professional and organizational characteristics and found that some personal variable of teachers' age, intelligence, socio-economic status, need satisfaction were co-relates of job satisfaction, whereas professional characteristics of a teacher did not act as a co-relate of job satisfaction. Eight out of eleven organizational characteristics appeared as co-relates of job satisfaction, whereas personal and organizational characteristics jointly were better predictors of job satisfaction than when taken separately.

Srivastav (1986) measured job satisfaction and professional honesty of primary school teachers and reported that the primary school teachers had high job satisfaction and professional honesty. Female teachers as compared to male teachers, unmarried teachers as compared to married teachers, urban teachers as compared to rural teachers and non-agricultural family occupation background teachers were significantly higher in job satisfaction and professional honesty. Young teachers as compared to old teachers, junior teachers as compared to senior teechers and high academic achiever teacher as compared to low achiever teachers had also significantly higher job satisfaction, while caste did not have a significant effect on job satisfaction. The major factors of job dissatisfaction among the primary teachers were inadequate salary, lack of physical facilities, problems in getting arrears, exploitation by officer, etc. while professional honesty was higher than job satisfaction of primary school teachers.

Padmanabhaiah (1986) studied job satisfaction and teaching effectiveness of secondary school teachers and found that teachers in general were dissatisfied with their jobs. All the personal and demographic variables, except the variable 'qualification of teachers' could significantly influence the level of satisfaction with various job factors but not the total job satisfaction. Sex and place of working had no significant impact on level of job satisfaction of teachers, but teachers working in high schools were significantly more dissatisfied with physical facilities than those working in junior colleges, while married and unmarried teachers were significantly different in their level of job satisfaction.

Ramakrishnaih (1989) designed to make an in-depth study of job satisfaction of college teachers in relation to variables like attitude towards teaching, management, sex, personality, etc. and found that teachers in general, were satisfied with their job, whereas, teachers working in junior colleges, were less satisfied than those working in degree colleges. The type of management, sex, qualifications, marital status, experience, age, size of family and personality factors did not have any significant influence on the over all job satisfaction of the college teachers.

Reddy (1989) assessed the level of job satisfaction and factor affecting job satisfaction of primary school teachers found that primary teachers were satisfied with their jobs, whereas women teachers were more satisfied with their jobs than male teachers qualified and young teachers were more satisfied with their jobs than middle aged teachers. There was significant difference between level of job satisfaction of teachers classified as high, middle and low on the basis of their attitude towards teaching.

Thanagosai (1990) compared job satisfaction and job dissatisfaction among faculty members at Six teachers' college in the Bangkok metropolitan area with respect to age, gender, length of experience, faculty and salary. The findings of this research were compared with previous studies of Vatthaisong (1982) and Karoonlanjakorn (1986), which measured job satisfaction among faculty members in the North-eastern part in the non-metropolitan areas of central Thailand. The findings of this study indicated that faculty members with high ages, high work experience, high salaries, high academic ranks, high levels of education, and high administrative positions were more satisfied with their jobs than faculty members with low ranking in these demographic variables. The results of this research were similar to Vattaisaong's inquiry and those of the present study were satisfied with their jobs in every aspect except salary, while Karoonlanjakorn's findings reported that no area of dissatisfaction was revealed. Because the factors described in Herzberg's theory were not the same as those determined in this study. Herzberg's two factors theory may not be suitable for use with Thai faculty members in Thailand.

Sarma (1991) attempted to investigate the administrative behaviour of principals, the job satisfaction of teachers and students' academic achievement and found a positive relationship between principal's administrative behaviour and teachers' job satisfaction, while a low and non-significant relationship existed between principals' administrative behaviour and students' achievement. The job satisfaction among college teachers was moderately high, whereas no significant relationship existed between the job satisfaction of college teachers and students' achievement. There existed a relationship between the age of the teachers and job satisfaction and professional experience of teachers. Whereas teachers irrespective of sex, type of management, course of study, professional experience, age and marital status had the same opinion about job satisfaction.

Rawat (1992) studied the job satisfaction and value pattern of secondary school teachers and found that female were more satisfied with their jobs than male teachers. Sex, locality, type of organization and grade of teachers very feebly affected their value pattern, whereas job expectation, job reality and job satisfaction showed strong positive relationship with humanistic, creative knowledge, social and aesthetic values and negative relationship with political and economic values of a teacher.

Abraham (1994) made an attempt to study the nature of relationship between levels of job satisfaction, teacher effectiveness and length of service, tenure among college teachers and found that teacher who had high and medium level of job satisfaction were more effective teachers than those with low level of job satisfaction. Teachers differed significantly among themselves on their effectiveness and job satisfaction.

Chandraiah (1994) attempted to study the job satisfaction of teachers as an effect of age and found that the middle aged and older aged teachers were more satisfied with their jobs as compared to the younger group of teachers. The middle aged and older aged teachers did not differ in their job satisfaction. It was also observed that co-efficient obtained for the subjects, age and job satisfactions, tenure of service were all positive and significant.

Das and Panda (1995) attempted to find out job satisfaction of college teachers and higher secondary teachers in terms of sex and experience and found no significant difference in the degree of job satisfaction of college and higher secondary teachers. No significant difference was observed between male and female college teachers, male and female higher secondary teachers, female college and higher secondary teachers, experienced college and higher secondary teachers, inexperienced college and higher secondary teachers on their job satisfaction. It was also noticed that experienced college as well as higher secondary teachers did not have better job satisfaction than inexperienced college and higher secondary teachers respectively.

Auskar (1996) attempted to study the job satisfaction among teachers working in government and private secondary schools and found that most of the teachers were satisfied with their jobs. Teachers working in both government and private schools, were more satisfied with factors like promotion, recognition, independence salary, job security, work itself, job status and educational policies, whereas teachers working in private schools were more satisfied with factors like responsibility, achievement, working conditions and personal life.

Sudhira (1996) examined the job satisfaction and job stress of secondary school physical education teachers working in different management schools and found that the physical education teachers working in different management schools differed significantly on their job satisfaction, whereas physical teachers working in private schools had significantly higher job satisfaction as compared to teachers working in semi government and government schools. The teachers working in semi government schools were more satisfied than teachers of government schools.

Harper (1997)research study examined five organizational factors (participation, support, role conflict, role ambiguity and work load) and their relationship as predictors of job satisfaction and found that teachers' job satisfaction was predicted at least partially by organizational factors, whereas job satisfaction was predicted by participation, role conflict and support and intrinsic job satisfaction was predicted by role ambiguity, participation, work load and role conflict.

Owen (1997) conducted a study to determine if a significant relationship existed between job satisfaction of secondary school principal and the independent variables of income, district size, building size, average hours worked per week, years of experience as a principal, level of education, gender and age and found that those variable showing statistical significance were years of experience as an educator, income, level of education, district support and age.

Rutebuks (1997) studied the degree of teachers' job satisfaction and its relationship to commitment and selected work conditions and found teachers were generally satisfied with their jobs. Teachers' commitment to the teaching profession was highly related to job satisfaction among male teachers, whereas commitment to Church organization was highly related to job satisfaction among female teachers. Personal significance was more highly related to teachers' job satisfaction than any other work condition, especially female teachers and male teachers considered adult social interaction more important for job satisfaction.

Smith (1997) studied to determine if a relationship existed between teachers' level of involvement in decision making and their job satisfaction and found a significant relationship between the middle school teachers' level of involvement in decision making and their degree of job satisfaction. Those middle school teachers who were the most involved in decision making process were the most involved in decision making process were the most satisfied with their jobs.

Nazir (1998) measured overall job satisfaction of checks identified some determinants of job satisfaction and evaluated the perceived importance of job and background factors on overall job satisfaction. Duration of work was perceived as the most important factor determining job satisfaction followed by nature of work and relation with co-workers Promotion opportunities and management policy was the least important determinants of job satisfaction. Overall job satisfaction was higher for those Ss who considered job components as most important. Among background variables income and level of education were associated with job-satisfaction Long hours of work, inadequate wages, management policy, ability under utilization and lack of recognition were reported as the most important causes of job satisfaction.

Hanna Shachar (1999) investigated effect of school change project on teacher's satisfaction with their work and their perceptions of teaching difficulties. He concluded that: (*i*) teachers satisfaction remained stable over the period of the study while their statements of dissatisfaction referring primarily from their inability to reach their students and motivate them, declined significantly from the pre-test to the post-test; (*ii*) distinct differences were found between schools in teachers' expression of satisfaction and dissatisfaction with theirs work.

Joshi (1999) investigated the interrelationship between job-satisfaction, job involvement and work involvement and their relationship with age, job experience, monthly income and educational level. Results revealed a significant positive association between job satisfactions and job involvement. Employees' age, job experience and monthly income were significantly correlated with job involvement. Job satisfaction was significantly correlated only with monthly income.

Annamalai (1999) studied job satisfaction of teachers in relation to certain selected variables. The results show that the job-satisfaction scores of teachers were not found significantly different when compared on the basis of sex, education level marital status family structure, school level, age group and duration of school.

Fay Rodgers-Jenkinson and others (2000) studied Job satisfaction of Jamaican elementary school teachers. The findings indicate that the quality of school, working conditions and respondents. Relationship with other teachers was significantly related to satisfaction for both government and private school teachers. School prestige and parental encouragement were also significant predicators for public school teachers, leadership style, organizational structure and teacher-parent relationship predicated job satisfaction for private school teachers.

Tahira (2000) studied job satisfaction of secondary school teachers in relation to their personal variables, sex, experience, professional training, salary and religion and found that female teachers were more satisfied than their counterparts. A perceptible and significant difference exists in job satisfaction between groups of teachers differing in their experience, in favour of young teachers. It was also found teachers drawing less salary were more satisfied than those getting more salary and untrained teachers were more satisfied than trained one. Teachers belonging to Hindu community were more satisfied than Muslim teachers, but the difference was not significant.

Khatoon and others (2000) studied job satisfaction of secondary school teachers in relation to their personal variables sex, experience, professional training, salary and religion. Results reveal the majority of teachers liked their jobs. The female teachers had a greater degree of job satisfaction than the male teachers. Fresher teachers drawing less salary were more satisfied than their seniors who were more experienced teachers drawing higher salaries. Teachers training was found to influence negatively, whereas religion was not found to make any effect on the teachers' job satisfaction.

Beegam and Dharmangadan (2000) examined gender differences in job satisfaction in a sample of 415 college teachers (age 23-55 years) with an equal number of males and females. Female teachers were more satisfied with their jobs than male teachers.

Pattanayak (2000) studied the effects of shift work and hierarchical positions in the organization on job satisfaction and perceived organizational commitment of 360 employees of the Rourkela Steel Plant. The nature of duty as well as the hierarchical position of employees influenced organizational commitment. Both executives and supervisors in shift and non-shift areas experienced an almost similar level of job stress in a number of dimensions. With regard to the HRD climate, there was a significant difference between shift and non-shift employees irrespective of their job category.

Bhatt (2001) attempted to find out relationship among the teachers' job stress, job involvement and their job satisfaction on 16 factors and found that the teachers' job stress was significantly and negatively associated with job involvement and job satisfaction whereas job involvement was highly significantly and positively correlated with the teachers' job satisfaction. Four factors of job stress were significantly negatively correlated with their overall job satisfaction. There existed a negative insignificant partial correlation between teachers job stress and job satisfaction.

Panda (2001) studied job-satisfaction of dot-com executives at various levels from content managers to vice presidents. Most of the Ss were satisfied with the job they were doing but dissatisfied with their present organization. The nature and content of the job was the driving force behind satisfaction, whereas apprehensions and operational problems about long-term survival of the company were indicators of dissatisfactions. Salary was rated as the most important factor contributing to job satisfaction in dot-com companies. The nature of the job with scope for creative executive was ranked higher for providing satisfaction as compared to job security. Extended working hours and fear of loss of job led to maximum dissatisfaction. Also, job satisfaction had a negative correlation with job status.

Antony (2002) studied exploring the satisfaction of part time college faculty in the United States. The result states that part-time college faculty experience different levels of satisfaction with workload, job-security, advancement opportunities, pay or benefits. Contrary to popular perceptions, PTF members report more overall satisfaction with theirs jobs than do full-time faculty PTF would be most likely to leave their present positions for a greater opportunity to teach.

Cote and others (2002) studied a longitudinal analysis of the association between emotion regulation, job-satisfaction and intentions to quit. This study shows that: (*a*) suppression of unpleasant emotions decreases job-satisfaction, which in turn increases intentions to quit; and (*b*) the amplification of pleasant emotions increase job-satisfaction.

Yousef (2002) studied job-satisfaction as a mediator of the relationship between role stressors and organizational commitment: A study from an Arabic cultural perspective. Results reveal that job-satisfaction directly and positively related to continuance commitment-low perceived alternatives. Both role conflict and role ambiguity directly and indirectly influenced job-satisfaction. It was found that job-satisfaction mediated the influences of role-conflict, and role ambiguity on various facets of organizational commitment, except continuance commitment-high personal sacrifice.

To conclude, these studies clearly show that the teachers' job satisfaction was directly or indirectly affected by role conflict, emotion, quality of school, role ambiguity and inability to reach their students and motivate them. Background factors like income, level of education, lack of recognition, management policy, working conditions, relationship with other colleagues and job stress have effect on job satisfaction.

STUDIES RELATED TO PROFESSIONAL COMMITMENT

Rizer and Trice (1969), Ferris and Aranya (1983) and Stabl et al. (1979) have reported positive correlation between professional commitment and organizational commitment whereas Welsh and Lavan (1981) found no significant relationship between organizational commitment and professional commitment.

Mathur (1981) studied mobility patterns and professional commitment of higher secondary school women teachers of Delhi. The findings are: (1) There was positive relationship between mobility and professional commitment; (2) Normally teachers did not like unnecessary transfers and changes of schools. A majority of mobility patterns were negatively correlated with professional commitment of women teachers except for some personal reasons when teachers opted for a change of places mobility had no negative influence; (3) Upward mobility was positively related with professional commitment; (4) Upward mobility in the same school was most conducive to professional commitment; and (5) Lack of mobility was least conducive to professional commitment.

Rana (1981) studied professional commitment of home science college teachers in India and its relationship to personal and professional characteristics and to organizational climate The findings were: (*i*) a majority of the home Science college teachers had a moderate level of value commitment and continuance commitment to teaching; (*ii*) value commitment which implied interest in teaching for its own sake, was predominant in the professional commitment of a majority of the home science teachers; (*iii*) The pattern of characteristics of the teachers with a high level of continuance commitment; (*iv*) a majority of the home science college and university departments had an often-organizational climate. Value commitment and continuance commitment to teaching was not significantly associated with the organizational climate.

Rusbult and Farrel (1983) reported from their study that though job satisfaction and job commitment was related to each other. In general, job satisfaction resulted from high job rewards, low job costs whereas job commitment was produced by high rewards, low costs, poor alternatives and large investment size was found to exert a greater impact on job commitment. With passage of time they argued that process of decline in job commitment proceeded and showed most direct and powerful effect on decisions to leave the job.

Pandey (1986) studied organizational commitment, professional commitment and job involvement in relation to the organizational climate, micro job climate and personality variables on 424 scientists working in R&D of a big Research Organization. Multiple regression analysis revealed weak predictive nature of organizational and job climate variable on professional commitment but personality (growth and work environment) variables were found to be strong predicators.

Bisaria (1991) studies mobility pattern and professional commitments of higher secondary teachers. The findings were: (1) the general scheme of transfers after a certain length of stay at one school was not conducive to commitment. In fact, frequent transfers and a majority of the mobility patterns were negatively correlated to professional commitment, if transfers were done only after an assessment of the performance of teachers; (2) Upward mobility was conducive to professional commitment but downward and horizontal mobility were negatively correlated with professional commitment.

Riketta (2002) studied attitudinal organizational commitment and job performance: A Meta analysis. He estimated that the true correlation between attitudinal organizational commitment and job performance and to identify moderators of this correlation. The correlation was at least marginally significantly stronger for: (*a*) extra-role performance as opposed to in role performance; (*b*) white collar workers as opposed to blue-collar workers; and (*c*) performance assessed by self-ratings as opposed to supervisor ratings or objective indicators. Four other assumed moderators (commitment measures. Affective commitment scale versus organizational commitment Questionnaire, job level, age and tenure) didn't have at least marginally significant effects.

Jernigam (2002) studied dimensions of work satisfaction as predictors of commitment type. The result indicated that satisfaction with professional status was a significant predictor of moral commitment. Dissatisfaction with organizational policies, autonomy, and professional status were significantly predictors of alienative commitment. None of the dimensions of work satisfaction were predictors of calculative commitment. The results of this study suggest that understanding how various factors impact the nature and the form of individual's organizational commitment is worth the effort. It is argued that if managers do not know what causes an attitude to take on a particular firm, they can't accurately predict what behaviour might be.

Pattanayak (2002) studied effects of shift-work and hierarchical position in the organizational of psychological correlates: A study on an integrated Steel Plant. He examined the dependent variable like job satisfaction perceived organizational commitment, job stress and HRD climate between shift and non-shift employee's vis-à-vis executives and non-executives. The findings reveal that there is significant interaction effect on total organizational commitment, job integration and challenge, trust and confidence, role ambiguity and role overload. Non-Shift employees experiencing higher job stress lowered organizational commitment and also perceiving HRD climate in a less favourable manner compared to the shift employees.

Snape and others (2003) studied an evaluation of a three-component model of occupational commitment: Dimensionality and consequences among United Kingdom human resource management specialists. Findings suggest that the consequence of the affective, normative and continuance components differ. Affective and continuance commitment were negatively related to occupational withdrawal cognition, whereas normative commitment was negatively related to withdrawal cognition only when continuance commitment was low. Affective and to a lesser extent, normative commitment were related to intention to participate in professional activities. Continuance commitment has no significant relationship with intention to participate in professional activities.

Stingthamber and others (2003) studied organizations and supervisors as sources of support and targets of commitment: A longitudinal study. They examined the linkages between the favourableness of intrinsically and extrinsically satisfying job-conditions, perceived organizational support, perceived supervisors' support, affective commitment to the organization and supervisor and turnover. Affective Commitment to the supervisor was found to completely mediated the effect of perceived supervisors support on turnover, whereas neither perceived organizational support nor organizational affective commitment were significantly related to turnover. Perceived organizational support partially mediated the effect of favourable intrinsically satisfying job conditions on organizational affective commitment and fully mediated the effect of extrinsically satisfying job conditions on organizational affective commitment. Finally, perceived supervisor support totally mediated the effect of favourable intrinsically satisfying job conditions on affective commitment to the supervisor.

The above Indian and foreign studies reveal that job commitment and job satisfaction were related to each other. Satisfactions resulted from high job and rewards, low job costs. Frequent transfers and mobility pattern were negatively correlated to professional commitment. Upward mobility was conducive to professional commitment but downward and horizontal mobility were negatively correlated with professional commitment. Personality (growth and work environment) variables were found to be strong predictors of professional commitment but organizational and job climate variables were weak predictors.

Overall Trends

The following observations may be made from studies reviewed for this study:

(*a*) There is a good deal of research that has been done on occupational stress, job satisfaction and professional commitment in different organizations, companies, industrial sector, health and banking sectors.

(*b*) These researches have attempted to study a variety of issues including mental health, job performance, organizational climate, job involvement and mobility pattern etc.

(*c*) A variety of educational organizations have been studied including secondary schools, colleges (private and government) and universities. But elementary education is completely neglected by researchers in this area.

(*d*) Though a number of studies have been done in companies to see the effect of these variables on productivity yet in education primary level which is the most important field, is lagging behind especially in relation to teachers working in tribal areas.

So, the investigator is eager to study the occupational stress, job satisfaction in relation to professional commitment and background factors of primary school teachers in tribal areas, as there is dearth of studies in this area in primary education.

Statement of the Problem

Introduction

The selection of the problem in a research normally leads to the statement of the problem as its next aspect. A specific explanation to the problem is required to device a reasonable method of procedure to halt at retype of conclusions. It is for this purpose, the operational definitions of the term of the problem are needed to be defined. Further, it helps to move on the specific aspect from a general aspect of the problem. Hypothesis assists to link the theory and observation and vice versa of the problem. Hypothesis of the study, with clear objectives, helps to identify the variables involved in the study and guide the methodological procedure that can be employed.

Justification of the Study

Education is the basic necessity like food, clothes and shelter. But our country is lagging behind to provide this basic necessity in spite of its efforts. The literacy rate in most states has not been found satisfactory even after five decades since independence. The situation is worse in tribal areas. Although the number of primary schools has increased 2.82 times since 1951 and enrolments have improved, yet the responsibility of the government by creating a satisfactory infrastructure has in practice not been matched by corresponding outlays. Primary education in India is not only suffering from inadequate allocation of resources but there is also lacking proper management and organization. Teachers are much maligned but not much attention has been given in research to the status and role, the concerns and anxieties, the satisfaction and dissatisfactions of Indian teachers in the face of growing criticism, social pressure and poor economic returns. In the face of growing public criticism, there is a need to try to understand why young enthusiastic teachers turn into bored and aloof professionals in a few years time, why many of our teachers are apathetic and uninvolved and make no effort to improve their scholarship while some others placed in the same milieu are enthusiastic, committed and show a constant desire to grow professionally. We should be concerned about the potential consequences that declining public confidence in education in general and the teaching community in particular may have on the self-esteem and the professional self-image of the teachers.

There are few professions like teaching that are open to intense public scrutiny because most of the schools are maintained by public money, funds from Central, State or Local Government, religious bodies or charitable organizations. There is also a constant flow of information from students to their parents, more so in urban areas, where parents themselves are likely to be educated and more concerned about the education of their wards.

It has been estimated that teachers typically make more than four hundred decisions a day. They dispense acceptance, rejection, praise and reproof on a whole scale basis. Many occupations or professions are distinct on this point from teaching. It is sobering to think that any one of these decisions may have either a short or long-range positive or negative influence upon a given student.

Teachers in India are increasingly facing a condescending attitude from both pupils and parents in rural, urban and tribal areas. That is why the investigator was anxious to investigate stress in teaching—what are the determinants of occupational stress, why teachers are not satisfied with their job, why teachers are not committed to their occupation. This is a matter of great concern as the teacher is the centre of the grand opera of teaching learning and the whole system revolves around him.

Primary school teachers particularly in tribal areas face a lot of stresses in teaching. In tribal areas, there are many factors like poor facilities, lack of advancement, uncongenial working conditions, handling disinterested students, local language barriers etc. Due to these stresses, teachers want to migrate from tribal areas to other areas, take leave showing false reasons and moreover, irregular attendance of the teachers is seen in many schools. That is why the investigator wants to get answers to the following questions especially related to teachers working in tribal areas:

- Do the teachers face stress in teaching?
- Are the teachers satisfied with their occupation?
- Are the teachers committed to their profession?

If the teachers are not free from stress, and are not satisfied and committed to their profession, then the causes shall be found out. On the basis of the findings of these questions, policy makers, government and educationists will possess strong background to provide better educational system for the country's upliftment.

Statement of the Problem

In the light of aforesaid considerations, the topic formulated was stated as under:

"OCCUPATIONAL STRESS AND JOB SATISFACTION IN RELATION TO PROFESSIONAL COMMITMENT AND BACKGROUND FACTORS IN PRIMARY SCHOOL TEACHERS OF TRIBAL AREAS".

OPERATIONAL DEFINITIONS OF THE TERMS USED

Occupational Stress

Occupational stress is the stress, which employees perceive arising from various constituent and conditions of their job. Here, some factors of the job life which cause stress in some way or the other are role overload, role ambiguity, role conflict, group and political pressures, responsibility for persons, under participation, powerlessness, poor peer relations, intrinsic improvement, low status, strenuous working condition and un profitability.

Job-Satisfaction

Job-satisfaction is an attitude, which results from balancing and summation of many specific likes and dislikes experiences in connection with job. In this study, the major factors of the job-satisfaction of teachers are: (*a*) intrinsic aspect; (*b*) salary, service conditions and promotion; (*c*) physical facilities; (*d*) institutional plans and policies; (*e*) satisfaction with authorities; (*f*) social status and family welfare; (*g*) rapport with students; and (*h*) relationship with co-workers.

Professional Commitment

Professional commitment means the consistency in the lines of actions undertaken regarding any profession. Consistency in teaching profession is called professional commitment of teachers. Commitment of teachers can be measured from following indicators:

(a) Positive Indicators: 1. Awareness of the duties of a teacher; 2. Academic competence and will to improve upon it; 3. Awareness of the latest methods of teaching i.e. professional competence and will to improve upon it; 4. Understanding of the child psychology; 5. Interest in the whole some development of the personality of the students; 6. Patience to and sympathy with the students; 7. Tactfulness and resourcefulness; 8. Punctuality and regularity; 9. Sincerity; 10. An idea of the management of time in order to cover the syllabus and do justice to each topic; 11. Able to control the class and maintain discipline;12. Commanding respect from the students; 13. Making efforts to keep in touch with the parents for the benefit of the students; 14. Helping in administrative work; 15. Helping in organizing co-curricular activities; 16. Job-satisfaction and feeling of pleasure in performing role as a teacher; 17. Will to continue in the teaching profession; 18. A dependable and willing worker; 19. A person with strong character.

(b)Negative Indicators: 1. Refusal to take up more gainful job or occupation; 2. Sacrifice of one's own leisure time; 3. Sacrifice of money; 4. Minimization of one's own needs; 5. Neglect of one's own family; 6. Control over one's temper; 7. Sacrifice of one's own pleasure; and 8. Less critical of others.

Background Factors

The following background factors will be taken into consideration:

1. Sex
2. Size of family—Number of members dependent on the teacher
3. Teaching experience
4. Service in tribal areas
5. Socio-economic Status: In this study, educational qualification, income of the teacher's parents, spouse as well as the teacher himself is taken into consideration in socio-economic status.

Objectives of the Study

- To develop professional commitment scale for primary school teachers.
- To know the level of job-satisfaction, occupational stress and professional commitment of primary school teachers in tribal areas.
- To study the relationship between occupational stress and professional commitment in primary school teachers in tribal areas.
- To study the relationship between job-satisfaction and professional commitment in primary school teachers in tribal areas.
- To study the relationship between job satisfaction and occupational stress in primary school teachers in tribal areas.

- To study main and interactional effects of professional commitment on occupational stress among primary school teachers in relation to following background factors:
  - Sex
  - Marital status
  - Teaching experience
  - Service in tribal area
  - Family size
  - Socio-economic status

To study main and interaction effects of professional commitment on job-satisfaction in primary school teachers in relation to above background factors.

Hypotheses of the Study

On the basis of the objective of the study and scanning of the concerned literature, the following hypotheses were framed:

- The teachers in tribal areas have average level of occupational stress, job-satisfaction and professional commitment
- There exists positive significant relationship between occupational stress and professional commitment.
- There exists positive significant relationship between job-satisfaction and professional commitment.
- There exists significant relationship between job satisfaction and occupational stress.

There exist significant main and interactional effects of professional commitment on occupational stress among primary school teachers in tribal area in relation to following background factors:

- Sex
- Marital status
- Teaching experience
- Service in tribal area
- Family size
- Socio-economic status

There exist significant main and interactional effects of professional commitment on job satisfaction among primary school teachers in tribal area in relation to above background factors.

Delimitations of the Study

As human behaviour is a vast study, it can't be studied to global scale at a time. So, the researcher has to delimit the problem under investigation up to a certain extent, otherwise it is not possible to control all the factors involved in it The present study will be delimitated in its scope in the following aspects:

- The study will be confined to primary school teachers teaching in tribal areas of Orissa State;
- The study will be confined to study of occupational stress, job satisfaction, professional commitment and background factors of teachers;
- The sample will be limited to teachers in four tribal districts i.e. Bolangir, Sambalpur, Kandhamal, Koraput of Orissa (India).

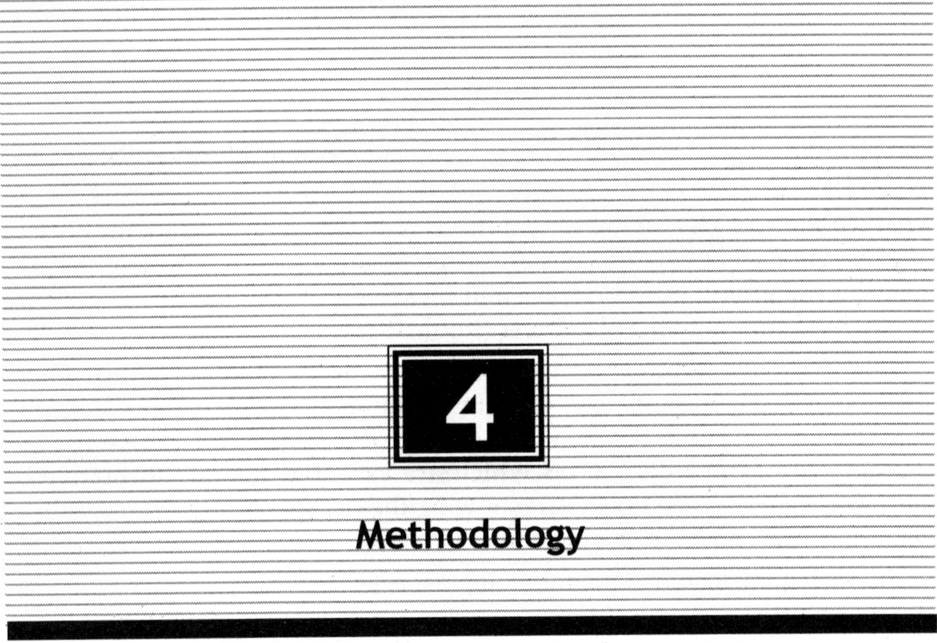

4

Methodology

Introduction

Normally the research study progresses with a systematic procedure and gain its end product, i.e. the outcome of the research study. In this process, the methods applied to arrive at the outcome, are the most essential one in the study. In fact a well scientifically planned systematic method logically takes to the approach to the best results. Hence the methodology is a crucial aspect in any research study.

Research methodology implies the research methods and considers the logic behind the methods that have been used in the context of any research study, what has been used, what data have been collected, what method is adopted, why a particular technique of analysing data is used, are answered in the methodology of a research study. This chapter presents a brief outline of the design of the study, the participants involved in the study, description of materials used for data collection and procedure followed to accomplish the study. The details of the variables and procedures have been described as accurately and completely as possible to facilitate the replication of the study by other researchers.

Design of the Study

Descriptive survey method of research was employed for the execution of the present study. Descriptive studies are designed to obtain pertinent and precise information regarding the current status of phenomena and to draw valid general conclusions from the facts discovered. So, these studies are not just collection of data but also involve measurement, classification, analysis, comparison and interpretation. They provide three types of information i.e. (*a*) of what exists with respect to variables or conditions in a situation; (*b*) of what we want by identifying set standards with which of compare the present conditions of what experts consider to be desirable and (*c*) how to achieve goals by explaining possible ways and means on the basis of the experience of others or the opinions of experts (Koul, 1988).

The present investigation is concerned with the study of occupational stress, job-satisfaction and professional commitment of primary school teachers in tribal areas and their background factors. Hence, all the steps and characteristics have been used which are essential for the normative or descriptive survey. The flow chart showing the design of the present study in detail has been given in this section.

This chapter includes the following aspects:

- Population and sample
- Description of the tools used
- Collection of data
- Scoring of the tools
- Categorization
- Statistical techniques used

Population and Sample

It is very essential on the part of the investigator to decide about the persons, groups or organizations or communities from whom she is going to collect the data. The way this decision is made will affect the conclusions, which may be drawn and the precision of these conclusions (Festinger and Katz, 1953).

According to Deighton (1971), "Sampling generally refers to the process of selecting a small part of specimen of something in order to determine some quality or characteristic of the whole." It is useful in many ways to select a smaller population representative of the larger universe under study. It not only saves time, energy and money of the investigator but also facilitates her to study the problem in hand intensively. Moreover, the collection of data of some phenomena in complete details would gather such a mass of data whose analysis would be slow and tedious. The analysis of large quantity of material may involve a number of errors, which would make the study useless, or the study may take so long that the importance of the study would be diminished when completed. So, it is always useful to take a smaller representation of the large whole.

The present study is confined to the primary school teachers in tribal areas of Orissa. Initially, Orissa was divided into thirteen districts but at present there are thirty districts in Orissa. Among them fully and partial tribal districts i.e. Bolangir, Sonepur, Kalahandi, Keonjhar, Koraput, Royagada,

Mayurbhanj, Kandhamal, Baudh, Sambalpur, Nabarangpur, Malkanagiri, Nuapada. The investigator decided to select sample from wholly as well as partially tribal districts for her study by applying randomized sampling method. Bolangir, Koraput, Kandhanal, Sambalpur, districts were selected for the study. Here, 400 teachers were selected for the sample.

Table 4.1 : No. of Teachers from Different Districts

Sr. No.	Name of the Districts	Number of Teachers
1.	Bolangir	88
2.	Sambalpur	111
3.	Kandhamal	110
4.	Koraput	91
	Total	**400**

Description of the Tools Used

Tools are selected for the collection of data keeping in mind the objectives of the study, variables undertaken for the study, dimensions of the variables etc. Taking into consideration of all these factors, the researcher decided to use the following tools:

(*a*) Occupational Stress Index by A.K. Srivastava and Dr. A.P. Singh

(*b*) Job Satisfaction Scale by Meera Dixit

(*c*) Professional Commitment Scale (Self prepared)

(*d*) Socio-economic Status Scale by S.N. Rao.

Occupation Stress Index (OSI)

The occupational stress index purports to measure the extent of stress that employees perceive arising from various constituent and conditions of their job.

The scale consists of 46 items, each to be rated on the five-point scale. Out of 46 items, 28 are 'true-keyed' and rest 18 are 'false-keyed'. The items are related to almost all relevant components of the job life which cause stress in some way or the other, such as, role over load, role ambiguity, role conflict, unreasonable group and political pressures, responsibility for persons, under participation powerlessness, poor peer relations, intrinsic impoverishment, low status, strenuous working conditions and profitability.

Table 4.2 gives an account of the items constituting various sub-scales of the OSI along with their indices of internal consistency.

Reliability

The reliability index ascertained by spit-half (odd-even) method and Cronbach's alpha coefficient for the scale as a whole was found to be 0.935 and 0.90 respectively. The reliability indices of the 12 sub scales were also computed by the split-half method. Table 4.3 records the obtained indices.

Table 4.2 : Sub-scales of Occupational Stress Index

Sl.No.	Sub Scale (Occupational Stressors)	Serial number of the items in the schedule	Range of rbis
1.	Role overload	1,13,25,36,44,46	0.30-0.46
2.	Role ambiguity	2,14,26,37	0.20-0.48
3.	Role conflict	3,15,27,38,45	0.36-0.53
4.	Unreasonable group and political pressure	4,16,28,39	0.21-0.52
5.	Responsibility for persons	5,17,29	0.30-0.57
6.	Under-participation	6,18,30,40	0.55-0.73
7.	Powerlessness	7,19,31	0.44-0.62
8.	Poor peer relations	8,20,32,41	0.24-0.49
9.	Intrinsic impoverishment	9,21,33,42	0.32-0.64
10.	Low status	10,22,34	0.48-0.63
11.	Strenuous working condition	12,24,35,43	0.40-0.62
12.	Unprofitability	11,23	0.48-0.57

Table 4.3 : Split-half Reliability of OSI Sub Scales

S.No.	Sub Scales	Reliability Index
1.	Role overload	0.684
2.	Role ambiguity	0.554
3.	Role conflict	0.694
4.	Unreasonable group and political pressure	0.454
5.	Responsibility for persons	0.840
6.	Under-participation	0.630
7.	Powerlessness	0.809
8.	Poor peer relations	0.549
9.	Intrinsic impoverishment	0.556
10.	Low status	0.789
11.	Strenuous working condition	0.733
12.	Unprofitability	0.767

The coefficient of correlation of Occupational Stress Index ranges from 0.45 to 0.84. So, it shows that OSI's correlation is very high. Hence, occupational stress Index tool is highly reliable.

Validity

The validity of the occupational stress index was measured by computing coefficients of correlation between the scale on the OSI and the various measures of job attitudes and job behaviour. The employees' scores on the OSI is likely to positively correlated with the scores on the measures of such work manifesting attitudinal and motivational and personality variables which have proved lowering or moderating the level of occupational stress. The coefficients of correlation between the scores on the OSI and the measures of job involvement (Lodhal and Kejner, 1965), work motivation (Srivastava, 1980); Ego-strength (Hasan, 1970) and job satisfaction (Pestonjee, 1973) were found to be –0.56 (N=225), –0.44 (N=200), –0.40 (N=205) and –0.51 (N=500) respectively. The correlation between the scores on the OSI and the measure of Job Anxiety (Srivastava, 1974) was found to be 0.59 (N=400).

Job Satisfaction Scale

Meera Dixit's job satisfaction scale's purpose is to measure job-satisfaction of primary and secondary teachers. It included 31 items related to four aspects, i.e. (*i*) satisfaction with work; (*ii*) satisfaction with salary and security; (*iii*) satisfaction with institutional plans and policies; and (*iv*) satisfaction with authorities. This scale could cover all the major factors of the job satisfaction of teachers in Indian schools. These factors are:

1. Intrinsic aspects
2. Salary, service conditions and promotion
3. Physical facilities
4. Institutional plans and policies
5. Satisfaction with authorities
6. Social status and family welfare
7. Rapport with students
8. Relationship with co-workers

Reliability

Reliability of the scale was determined by split half method. The test was first divided into two equivalent halves and the correlation calculated for these half tests. From the reliability of the half test, the self-correlation of the whole test was calculated by using Spearman-Brown prophecy formula. Test-retest method also showed high reliability, which is given in the following tables:

Table 4.4 : Reliability of the test by Split-half Method

Version of the Form	N	R	Index of Reliability
English Version	100	0.85	0.92
Hindi Version	100	0.87	0.93

Table 4.5 : Reliability of the test by Test-Retest Method

Version of the Form	N	R	Index of Reliability
English Version	100	0.75	0.86
Hindi Version	100	0.76	0.87

From the above two tables, it is clear that by both split-half and test-retest method, the co-efficient of correlation is very high. The tool for job-satisfaction is highly reliable.

Validity

Item validity (discrimination value) was found out by item-test correlation method using Pearson's 'r' taking 25 per cent highest scores and 25 per cent lowest scores and finally calculating 't' value for the items of Hindi and English version of the scale separately. The items, which were not significant had to be dropped in the final form. Initially there were 58 items of which 6 items had to be deleted, as they were not found to be discriminatory in item analysis. Distribution of the items in the final form was as follows:

Table 4.6 : Distribution of items in the final form of Job-Satisfaction Scale

	Job Factors	Item Nos.	No. of Items
	Intrinsic aspect of the job	1,11,25,30,35,46 and 52	7
	Salary, promotional avenues and service conditions	3,12,19,20,31,34,45 and 50	8
	Physical facilities	2,10,24,29,36,43,48,49 and 51	9
	Institutional plans and policies	4,13,26,38,40 and 47	6
	Satisfaction with authorities	5,14,21,27,32 and 41	6
F.	Satisfaction with social status and family welfare	8,9,17,18 and 23	5
G.	Rapport with students	7,15,22,28,33 and 39	6
H.	Relationship with co-workers	6,16,37,42 and 44	5
	Total		**52**

Professional Commitment Scale

The investigator herself developed professional commitment scale. First of all, she prepared 98 items pertaining to the professional commitment on the basis of related literature, journals, books and the information gathered during the pilot study. But the investigator prepared the items mainly referring to index of commitment as stated by Backer. These 98 items were given to the educationists and language experts for vetting. The preliminary draft of the tool was modified and some of the items rejected in the light of suggestions given by the faculty members of the Kurukshetra University. So, lastly 50 items were kept in the preliminary draft.

Try-out

These 50 items were administered to 100 primary teachers of the same area from which final data collection was to be done for the present study. After collection of data and scoring of the preliminary scale, the investigator arranged the subjects in descending order according to the magnitude of their scores. The top 27 per cent were selected as upper group and the bottom 27 per cent as lower group which were used for the item analysis. To find out the discrimination power of each item, test of significance was applied to scores of upper and lower group and t-values were calculated for each item in the scale. After t-test the items showing significance at 0.05 levels were retained and others were rejected. So, in this process 33 items were selected for the final draft of professional commitment scale.

Reliability

In the present study the scale was administered again after a gap of one month on same 100 teachers for the try-out. The reliability of the scale was computed by test-retest method. The correlation co-efficient between two sets of scores was calculated. It came out to be 0.82, which showed that the scale had high coefficient of stability.

Validity

The scale was given to the senior teachers in the field of psychology and education to read and judge the items. Finally content validity of the professional commitment scale was estimated by evaluating its relevance to instructional objectives and actual subject matter studied.

Further, intrinsic validity of the scale was determined by calculating the square root of the reliability coefficient. It came out to be 0.90, which showed that the present scale had high intrinsic validity co-efficient. Thus, the scale can be taken to be having high level of reliability and validity coefficients.

Socio-economic Status

To assess the socio-economic status of the subjects, Rao's Socio-economic status scale was adopted. This scale hás an advantage over other scales like that of Kuppuswamy (1962) and Pareek and Trivedi (1964) because it can be used with persons coming from all the areas viz. urban, semi-urban and rural. Studies conducted by Vashistha (1981), Panda (1981) and Ram Pal (1983) reported that the Rao's scale is more objective than other scales. According to them, the scale is more promising in bringing comprehensive picture of economic conditions. All these studies have been conducted on adolescents or college students. But in the present study, the sample consisted of persons who have already attained a particular status. In order to make this scale suited for such persons, it was thought imperative to modify the Rao's scale as per sample subjects. Educational level of the members of the family, total income of the family from all sources and occupation of family members of the teachers were considered to compute S.E.S. of the teachers. Other items item relating to sibling position, locality, property etc. were not taken into account.

Further, the income slabs to give weightage to family income were modified in the light of the economic status of the people in general in the State of Orissa.

The Test-retest reliability of the scale has been found by using Spearman-Brown Prophecy formula. Reliability of the scale is 0.89.

COLLECTION OF DATA

The investigator visited the schools personally and administered the tools to the teachers with a request to give their responses against all the items of the tools separately. They were not only explained the purpose and significance of collecting required information from them but also made them clear that the information collected would be kept confidential and utilized for research purpose only. The teachers showed keen interest and involvement to go through each item sincerely and carefully. The investigator told the teachers to put tick mark (✓) against any of the five choices: SD (Strongly Disagree), D (Disagree), U (Undecided), SA (Strongly Agree) and A (Agree) for each statement as they think the most appropriate answer. The investigator convinced the unwilling teachers also about the purpose of the study and was successful in collecting data even from them.

SCORING PROCEDURE

Scoring of the Occupational Stress Index Scale

Since the questionnaire consists of both true keyed and false-keyed items, two different patterns of scoring have to be adopted for two types of items. The following table provides guideline to score the responses given in two categories of items:

Table 4.7 : Scoring of responses on Occupational Stress

Categories of response	Score for true-keyed	Score for false-keyed
Never/strongly disagree	1	5
Seldom/Disagree	2	4
Sometimes/undecided	3	3
Mostly/Agree	4	2
Always/Strongly agree	5	1

The total score obtained on all the items was taken as occupational stress index.

(b) Scoring of Job-Satisfaction Scale: Scoring is on a five-point scale from one to five (1 to 5). For the response of 'Strongly Agree' scoring is 1, for 'Agree' it is 2, for 'Undecided' 3 marks are allotted and for 'Disagree' scoring is 4 and for 'Strongly Disagree' it is 5. The job-satisfaction score was the summation of scores on all the items of the scale.

(c) Scoring of Professional Commitment Scale: Scoring weightage for positive statements is 1, 2,3,4,5 for Strongly Disagree, Disagree, Undecided, Agree and Strongly Agree respectively. Scoring weightage for negative statements is 5, 4,3,2,1 for Strongly Disagree, Disagree, Undecided, Agree and Strongly Agree respectively. The summated score on various item of the scale was taken as an index of professional commitment.

(d) Scoring of socio-economic status rating: The scoring of the socio-economic status of teachers was done according to the manual of directions and norms for the socio-economic status rating scale developed by Prof. S. Narain Rao as given in appendix-iv. Scoring weightage for education of siblings was used for scoring

CATEGORISATION

In the present study, investigator had categorized following variables for the study:

Professional Commitment

Professional commitment is categorized as high professional commitment and low professional commitment by calculating mean and standard deviation. High professional commitment was for those teachers who were above M + 1/2 SD and low professional commitment were for those teachers who come under M-1/2 SD.

Table 4.8 : Categorization of Professional Commitment Groups

Score	Category	Number of Teachers
M+1/2 SD or above(130 marks or above)	High P.C.	114
M-1/2SD(116 marks or less)	Low P.C.	122

(b)Socio-economic Status (SES) : SES was categorised as High SES, Middle SES and Low SES on the basis of calculating P33 and P66 of SES scores as shown below.

Table 4.9 : Categorization of Socio-economic Status Groups

Score	Category	Number of Teachers
P66 & Above(33 marks or above)	High SES	134
Between P33 & P66(Between 22 & 33 mark)	Middle SES	114
P33 and below (21 & less mark)	Low SES	152

(c) Family Size: Family Size was categorized as large family size and small family size by calculating median of family size scores as shown below:

Table 4.10 : Categorization of Family Size Groups

Score	Category	Number of Teachers
Above Median(More than 4 members)	Large Family size	236
Below Median(4 and Less than 4 members)	Small Family Size	164

(d)Teaching Experience: Teaching experience was also categorized as large teaching experience and less teaching experience by calculating median of teaching experience scores as shown below:

Table 4.11 : Categorization of Teaching Experience Groups

Score	Category	Number of Teachers
Above Median (Above 13 years)	More Teaching Experience	202
Below Median(13 years and less)	Less Teaching Experience	198

(e) Service in Tribal Area (STA): STA variable was categorized as long service in tribal area and short service in tribal area on the basis of calculating median of service in tribal area scores as shown below:

Table 4.12 : Categorization of Service in Tribal Area Groups

Score	Category	Number of Teachers
Above Median (Above 14 years)	Long STA	189
Below Median(14 Years and less)	Short STA	211

(f) Sex: Sex was divided into two levels i.e. male (257) and female (143)

(g) Marital Status: Marital Status of the teachers was categorized as married teachers (366) and unmarried teachers (34).

STATISTICAL TECHNIQUES USED

The researcher uses appropriate statistical techniques to make analysis on different types of score available for further comparisons to draw inferences.

For the present study ANOVA, Mean, SD, Median, P33, P66 and Interco-relation were applied for the purpose.

FLOW CHART SHOWING DESIGN OF THE STUDY

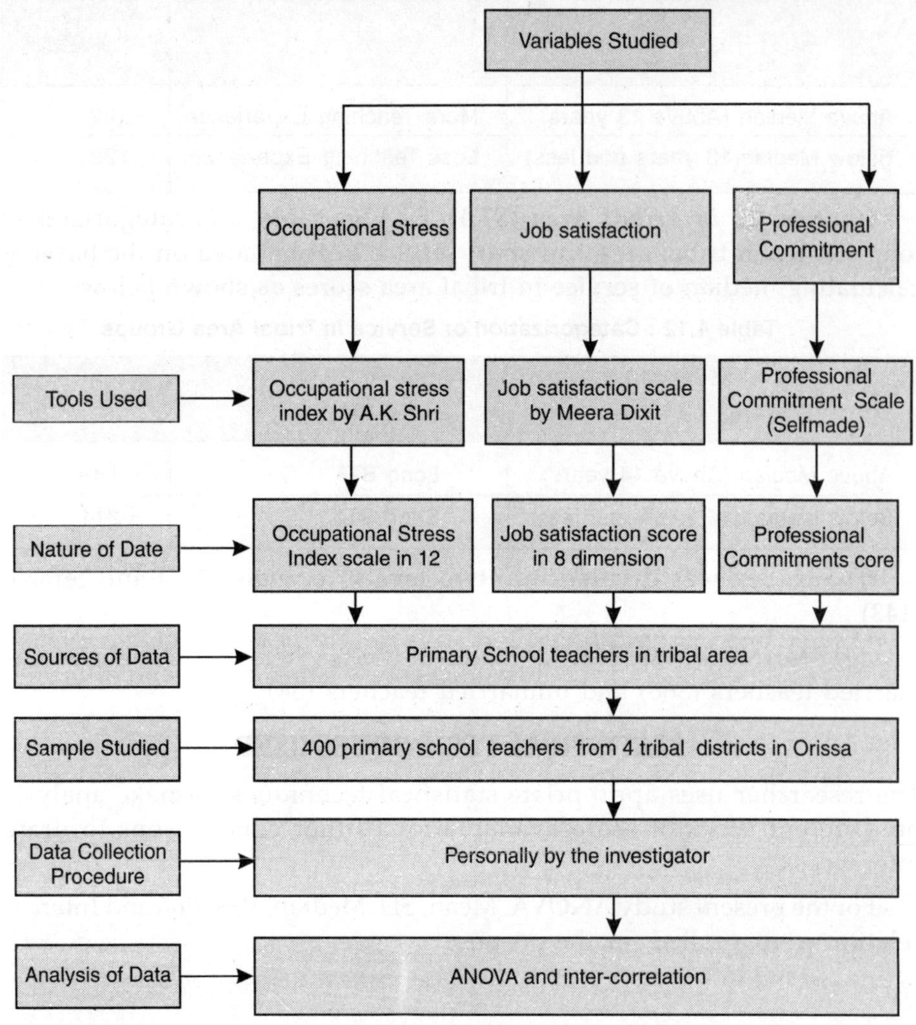

5

Analysis and Interpretation

Analysis of Data

For any worthwhile purpose, the data must be carefully edited, systematically classified and tabulated, scientifically analyzed, intelligently interpreted and rationally concluded. The researcher is able to get a meaningful conclusion out of raw information only after analysis of data. Analysis of data means studying the tabulated material in order to determine inherent facts or means. It breaks down existing complex factors into simpler parts and puts the parts together in new arrangements for the purpose of interpretation.

Statistical Techniques Used

The investigator dealt with the study of main and interactional effects of professional commitment on occupational stress among primary school teachers in tribal areas in relation to various background factors as well as the main and interactional effects of professional commitment on job satisfaction among primary school teachers in tribal areas in relation to various background factors. For this purpose, the investigator made use of three-way analysis of variance technique. Besides ANOVA, the investigator also studied the relationships between various variables by computing product moment correlation coefficients.

Before proceeding with the ANOVA and correlation technique, the investigator computed M, SD and SK & KU to know the nature of distribution of job satisfaction, occupation stress and professional commitment scores in the population.

The whole work is divided into three sections i.e. Section A, Section B and Section C. Section A is related to study of nature of distribution of occupational stress, job-satisfaction and professional commitment of primary school teachers working in the tribal area; Section B consists of three sub-sections dealing with ANOVA Section C deals with inter-correlations. The detail of the result is given below:

Section A: Nature of distribution of occupational stress, job-satisfaction and professional commitment of primary school teachers working in tribal area.

Table 5.1 describes the nature of distribution of occupational stress, job-satisfaction and professional commitment scores of primary school teachers in tribal area.

Table 5.1 : Nature of data in Job Satisfaction score, Occupational Stress and Professional Commitment

Variables	M	SD	SK	Ku
JS	163.65	29.80	0.75	0.242
OS	150.875	24.81	0.74	0.232
PC	122.97	14.43	0.65	0.231

Table 5.2 : Showing norms of Job-Satisfaction based on percentile value for the scores of primary school teachers

Raw scores for primary teachers	Percentile value	Interpretation
93	0	Very low degree of satisfaction
102	1	
138	10	
146	20	Low degree of satisfaction
150	25	
154	30	
161	40	Average degree of satisfaction
167	50	
173	60	
181	70	Good degree of satisfaction
186	75	
190	80	
202	90	Highest degree of satisfaction
232	99	
240	100	

INTERPRETATION

The calculated value of Skewness and Kurtosis of job-satisfaction scores (0.75, 0.242) are less than the table value at 0.05 levels of significance. So, they are insignificant. That means job-satisfaction scores are normally distributed.

The calculated mean value of job-satisfaction scores (163.65) of primary school teachers in tribal falls in the category of 161-173(Table 5.2), which shows primary school teachers in tribal area have average degree of job-satisfaction. This average degree of job-satisfaction may be due to lack of physical facilities, lack of rapport with students, lack of satisfaction with social status and other stress in tribal area. The hypothesis of average level of job-satisfaction of primary school teachers in tribal area is accepted.

Table 5.3 delineates norms of three categories of occupational stress i.e. high, moderate and low level of occupational stress.

Table 5.3 : Levels of Occupational Stress

Sub-scales	Levels of occupational stress		
	Low (Below-1σ)	Moderate (Between ± 1σ)	High (Above ± 1σ above)
I	6-14	15-22	23-30
II	4-9	10-12'	13-20
III	5-12	13-17	18-25
IV	4-9	10-14	15-20
V	3-7	8-11	12-15
VI	4-9	10-12	13-20
VII	3-7	8-11	12-15
VIII	4-8	9-13	14-20
IX	4-9	10-13	14-20
X	3-6	7-11	12-15
XI	4-9	10-12	13-20
XII	2-4	5-7	8-10
Scale as a whole	46-122	123-155	156-230

INTERPRETATION

The calculated value of Skewness and Kurtosis of occupational stress scores (0.74 and 0.232) are less than the table value at 0.05 levels of significance. So, they are insignificant. That means occupational stress scores are normally distributed.

From table 5.1, the calculated (M±1σ) value of occupational stress scores of primary school teachers in tribal falls in the category of 123-155 and 156-230 (Table 5.3). So, it is inferred that primary school teachers in tribal area experience moderate to high level of occupational stress. This level of occupational stress may be due to role ambiguity, strenuous working condition, low status and poor peer relation etc. The hypothesis of average level of occupational stress of primary school teachers in tribal area is rejected.

The calculated Skewness and Kurtosis value of professional commitment scores (0.65 and 0.231) are less than the table value at 0.05 levels of significance. So, it is insignificant. That means professional commitment scores are normally distributed.

From table 5.1, it is evident that the calculated mean value of professional commitment (M=122.97) is much higher than the expected average value (M=99) of the scores. It shows that sampled teachers in primary schools in tribal areas have high level of professional commitment. The hypothesis of average level of professional commitment of primary school teachers in tribal area is rejected.

Advantages of ANOVA

Analysis of variance is an economical method and is used for testing the significance of means when groups are two or more than two. t-test is the simplest method to find out the differences in means separately from each group, which was very cumbersome for the investigator. Factorial design of analysis of variance is a statistical method that analyses differences and interactive effects of two or more independent variables on the dependent variable. Moreover, the study of interaction may provide with additional insight as to how each factor operates and how the interaction between any of the two factors differed at the different levels of the third factor. It also helps in manipulating and controlling two or more variables simultaneously. So the investigator selected this technique to arrive at suitable conclusion for its following advantages.

The possible significance of mean differences can be analysed by an overall test of significance when there are many results to be compared. It saves time and involves less risk of alpha error i.e., when we reject the null-hypothesis of small values to be significant at 0.05 level of confidence.

This method tends to lessen the risk of type-II error or beta error i.e. failing to reject false null-hypothesis by the use of a randomized block design. This is the case because the estimate of sampling error is when the variance associated with the differences among the means of blocks has been estimated from it. This advantage thus makes an increase in the power of the test of significance. It leads to higher values of variance of 'F' ratio and hence it increases the probability of rejection of false null hypothesis.

The important advantage of the ANOVA arises in the use of factorial design. The factorial experiment in its own turn has some merits. It is convenient in the following ways:

It brings to mind a summary of mass of statistical data in which the logical content of the whole is really appreciated.

Besides logical process, it is convenient in facilitating and reducing to a common form all the tests of significance which one wants to apply.

Another advantage is in the use of randomized block design. This design tends to lessen the risk of type-II error i.e. failing to reject the false null hypothesis.

Basic Assumptions of ANOVA

- Extent of soundness of deciding statistical technique depends upon how far certain assumptions have been satisfied in the data. For using analysis of variance, the following requirements are to be met:
- The sampling within the various tests should be random in the concerned variables. It usually means that observations are mutually independent and with equal chance of selection.
- The dependent variables should be normally distributed in the population from which samples have been drawn. Violation of this assumption makes the results appear somewhat more significant than what they actually are:
- The variances from within various sets must be approximately equal. The within sets mean square is commonly the denominator of F-ratios and consequently much depends upon its accuracy. Much variation among set variances leads to suspicion of an in accurate estimate of the population variance from within sets.
- The contribution to the total variance must be additive.

Testing Assumptions of ANOVA

- The assumption of randomness means that sampling within sets should be random which usually means observations are mutually independent and have equal opportunity to occur. It was amply fulfilled in this study at every stage wherever it was possible.
- The variations within experimentally homogenous sets should be from normally distributed population. However, Eden & Yates (Johnson, 1960) have shown that even with the populations departing considerably from normality, effectiveness of the F-distribution will still hold. Besides, on the basis of Norton's study, Guilford (1978) points out that one general finding was that 'F' test is rather insensitive to variations in the shape of population distribution.
- There are certain findings, which advocate that 'F' is somewhat sensitive only if variations in variances are serious. Therefore, even if the assumption of homogeneity is not fulfilled, one can apply 'Analysis of Variance'. According to Edward, "Box (1953) has pointed out that because the 'F' test was insensitive to non-normality and because with equal numbers, it was also insensitive to variance inequalities; it could be an accepted fact that it can be safely used under most of the conditions. In other words, F-test is a robust test, that it is relatively insensitive to violation of assumptions of normality of distribution and homogeneity of variance." Thus, satisfying the assumption of ANOVA, the researcher has presented the analysis of the data.

SECTION-B

Section B is further divided into three sub-sections depending upon the combination of independent variables.

Sub-Section—I

(*a*) Mean Differences in Job-Satisfaction in Relation to Professional Commitment, Sex and Marital Status

Here, two categories of sex i.e. male and female; two categories of marital status i.e. married and unmarried; two levels of professional commitment i.e. high professional commitment and low professional commitment were taken up. The basis of categorization has been given in chapter III. So, a 2x2x2 factorial design was prepared as follow:

Factorial Design

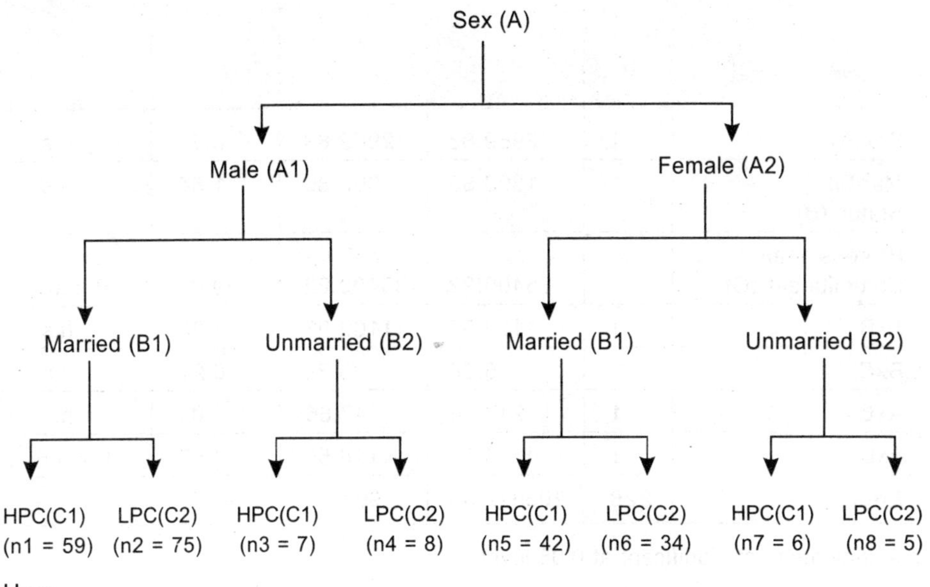

Here,

A1 = Male Teachers

A2 = Female Teachers

B1 = Married Teachers

B2 = Unmarried Teachers

C1 = High professional commitment Teachers

C2 = Low professional commitment Teachers

The mean job satisfaction scores in various cells of factorial design followed by summary of ANOVA results are given in tables 5.4 and 5.5.

Table 5.4 : Mean Job Satisfaction Scores of Teachers in relation to different category of professional commitment, sex and marital status

Groups	Male		Female	
	Married	Unmarried	Married	Unmarried
High P.C.	M1 =172.76	M2=174.71	M3=175.88	M4=205.67
Low P.C.	M5=149.07	M6=162.63	M7=156.18	M8=132.40

Mean score of high professional commitment teachers = 175.76

Mean score of low professional commitment teachers = 151.25

Table 5.5 : Summary showing Analysis of Variance on Job-Satisfaction Scores in relation to Professional Commitment, Sex and Marital Status (N=236)

Sources of Variation	Df	SS	MS	F-ratio	Level of significance
Sex(A)	1	2969.83	2969.83	3.27	n.s.
Marital Status (B)	1	1393.85	1393.85	1.54	n.s.
Professional Commitment (C)	1	35400.22	35400.22	39.01	P < .01
AxB	1	1162.93	1162.93	1.28	n.s.
BxC	1	6.38	6.38	0.27	n.s.
AxC	1	247.66	247.66	0.08	n.s.
AxBxC	1	4118.55	4118.55	4.57	P < .05
Error	228	206912.53	907.51	—	—

n.s. indicates not significant at 0.05 level.

INTERPRETATION

Main Effect

(1) Table 5.5 shows that F-ratio for the main effect of category of sex (A) at 1/228 df is less than the table value at 0.05 levels of significance. means that there exists no significant difference in job-satisfaction of male and female teachers. Thus, the hypothesis of significant difference in job-satisfaction of male and female teachers is not accepted.

(2) F-ratio for the main effect of marital status of the teachers (B) at 1/228 df is less than the table value at 0.05 level of significance. It means that there exists no significant difference in job-satisfaction of married and unmarried teachers. Thus, the hypothesis of significant difference in job-satisfaction of married and unmarried teachers is not accepted.

(3) F-ratio for the main effect of professional commitment (C) of teachers at 1/228 df is more than the table value at 0.01 level of significance. It means that there exists a significance difference in job-satisfaction of high professionally committed teachers and low professionally committed teachers. Thus, the hypothesis of significant differences in job-satisfaction of high professional commitment teachers and low professional commitment teachers is accepted.

Further, the mean values show that high professional committed teachers exhibit high job-satisfaction (M=175.76) than low professional committed teachers (M=151.25). Hence, professional commitment as a single main variable shows significant effect on job satisfaction.

Interactional Effects

(4) The calculated F-ratio for the two-factor interaction of category of Sex and Marital status (AxB) is less than the table value at 0.05 levels of significance. It means that the difference between the mean job-satisfaction scores of male teachers whether married or unmarried is not significantly different from the mean job-satisfaction scores of female teachers whether married or unmarried. Thus, the hypothesis of significant interaction between category of sex and marital status of teachers on their job satisfaction is not accepted.

(5) The calculated F-ratio for the two-factor interaction of category of Professional Commitment and Marital Status (BxC) is less than the table value at 0.05 levels of significance. This shows that the differences between the mean job satisfaction scores of married teachers whether high or low professional commitment is not significantly different from the mean job satisfaction scores of unmarried teachers whether high or low professional commitment. Thus, the hypothesis of significant interaction between marital status and professional commitment of teachers on their job satisfaction is not accepted.

(6) The calculated F-ratio for the two-factor interaction of Professional Commitment and Sex (AxC) is less than the table value at 0.05 levels of significance. This shows that the differences between the mean job satisfaction scores of male teachers whether high professional commitment or low professional commitment is not significantly different from the mean scores of female teachers whether high or low professional commitment. Thus, the hypothesis of significant interaction between professional commitment and sex of teachers on their job satisfaction is not accepted.

(7) The calculated F-ratio for the three-factor interaction of category of Professional Commitment, Sex and Marital Status of teachers (AxBxC) is more than the table value at 0.05 level of significance. So, the interactive effect of the three variables on job satisfaction of teacher is significant. This indicates that category of professional commitment; sex and marital status of teachers together reveal significant

differences on teachers' job–satisfaction. Hence, the hypothesis of significant triple interaction between category of professional commitment, sex and marital status of teachers on job-satisfaction is accepted. The same has been depicted graphically in Fig. 5.1.

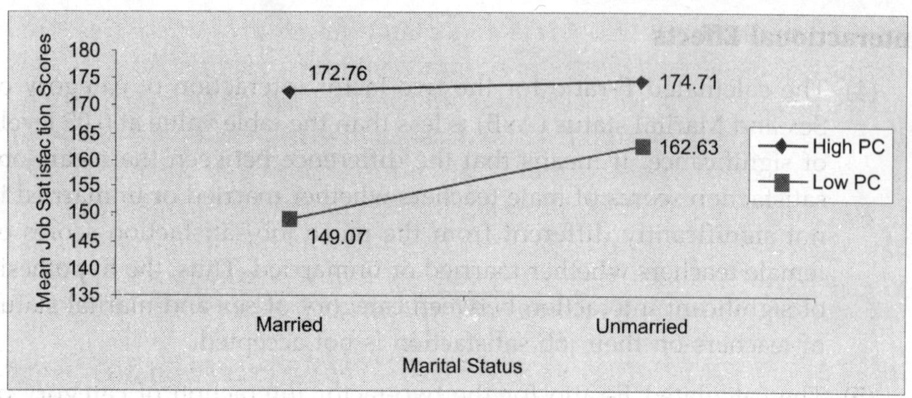

Fig. 5.1(a) Marital Status × Professional Commitment Interaction for Male Teachers

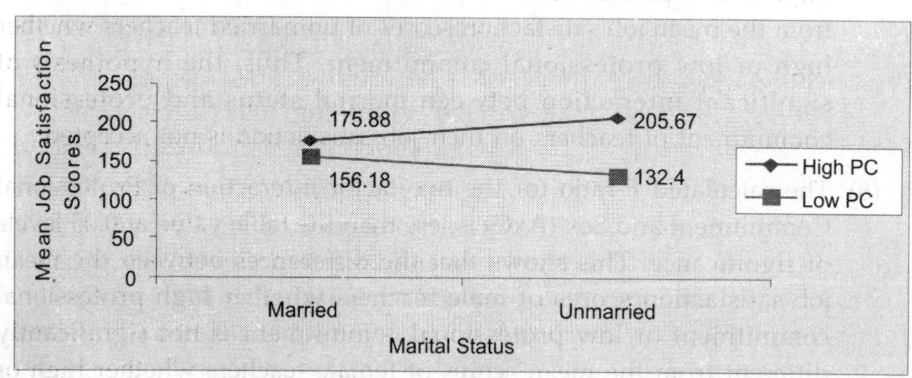

Fig. 5.1(b) Marital Status × Professional Commitment Interaction for Female Teachers

(*b*) Mean Differences in Occupation Stress In Relation to Profe-ssional Commitment, Sex and Marital Status

Mean scores in the area of occupational stress of male and female teachers belonging to high and low professional commitment as well as married and unmarried categories followed by summary of ANOVA are presented in Table 5.6 and 5.7 respectively.

Table 5.6 : Mean Occupational Stress Scores of Teachers in relation to category of Professional Commitment, Sex and Marital Status

Groups	Male		Female	
	Married	Unmarried	Married	Unmarried
High P.C.	M1 = 168.05	M2 =165.29	M3 =168.71	M4 =200.83
Low P.C.	M5 =142.32	M6 =137.00	M7 =142.09	M8 =131.00

Mean score of high professional commitment teachers = 169.85
Mean score of low professional commitment teachers = 141.44

Table 5.7 : Summary showing Analysis of Variance on Occupational Stress Scores of Teachers in relation to Professional Commitment, Sex and Marital Status (N=236)

Sources of Variation	Df	SS	MS	F-ratio	Level of significance
Sex (A)	1	1403.20	1403.20	2.73	n.s.
Marital Status (B)	1	267.74	267.74	0.52	n.s.
Professional Commitment (C)	1	47560.00	47560.00	92.41	P<0.01
AxB	1	1230.64	1230.64	2.39	n.s.
BxC	1	14.06	14.06	0.03	n.s.
AxC	1	220.32	220.32	0.43	n.s.
AxBxC	1	3789.86	3789.86	7.36	P<0.01
Error	228	117344.18	514.67	-	-

n.s. Indicates not significant at 0.05 levels.

INTERPRETATION

Main Effects

(1) Table 5.7 shows that F-ratio for the main effect of category of sex (A) at 1/228 df is less than the table value at 0.05 level of significance. It means that there exists no significant difference in occupational stress of male and female teachers. Thus, the hypothesis of significant difference in occupational stress of female and male teachers is not accepted.

(2) F-ratio for the main effect of marital status of teachers (B) at 1/228 df is less than the table value at 0.05 levels of significance. It means that

there exists no significant difference in occupational stress of married and unmarried teachers. Thus, the hypothesis of significant difference in occupational stress of married and unmarried teachers is not accepted.

(3) F-ratio for the main effect of professional commitment (C) at 1/228 df is more than the table value at 0.01 level of significance. It means that there exists significant difference in occupational stress of high professional committed and low professional committed teachers. Thus, the hypothesis of significant difference in occupational stress of high and low professional committed teachers is accepted.

Further, the mean values show that high professional committed teachers exhibit more occupational stress (M=169.85) than low committed teachers (M=141.44). Hence, professional commitment as s single main variable shows significant effect on occupational stress.

Interactional Effects

(4) The calculated F-ratio for the two-factor interaction of category of sex and marital status (A × B) is less than the table value at 0.05 levels of significance. It means that the difference between the mean occupational stress scores of male teachers whether married or unmarried teachers is not significantly different from the mean occupational stress scores of female teachers whether married or unmarried teachers. Thus, the hypothesis of significant interaction between category of sex and martial status of teachers on their occupational stress is not accepted.

(5) The calculated F-ratio for the two-factor interaction of category marital status and professional commitment (B × C) is less than the table value at 0.05 levels of significance. This shows that the difference between the mean occupational stress scores of married teachers whether high or low professional commitment is not significantly different from the mean occupational stress scores of unmarried teachers whether high or low professionally committed teachers. Thus, the hypothesis of significant interaction between marital status and professional commitment of teachers on their occupational stress is not accepted.

(6) The calculated F-ratio for the two-factor interaction of professional commitment and sex (A × C) is less than the table value at 0.05 levels of significance. This shows that the difference between the mean occupational stress scores of male teachers whether high or low professionally committed is not significantly different from the female teachers whether high or low professionally committed. Thus, the

hypothesis of significant interaction between professional commitment and sex of teachers on their occupational stress not accepted.

(7) The calculated F-ratio for the three-factor interaction of category of sex, marital status and professional commitment of teachers (A × B × C) is more than the table value at 0.01 levels of significance. So, the interactive effect of three variables on occupational stress of teachers is significant. This indicates that category of sex; marital status and professional commitment of teachers together reveal significant difference on teachers' occupational stress. Hence, the hypothesis of significant triple interaction between category of sex, marital status and professional commitment of teachers on occupational stress is accepted. The same has been depicted graphically in Fig. 5.2.

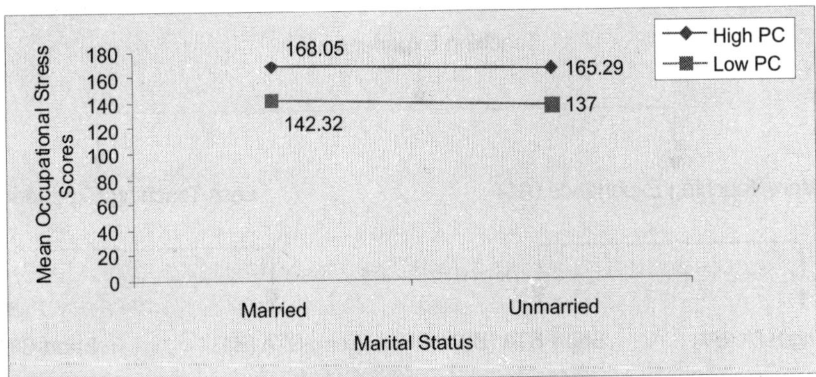

Fig. 5.2(a) Marital Status × Professional Commitment Interaction for Male Teachers

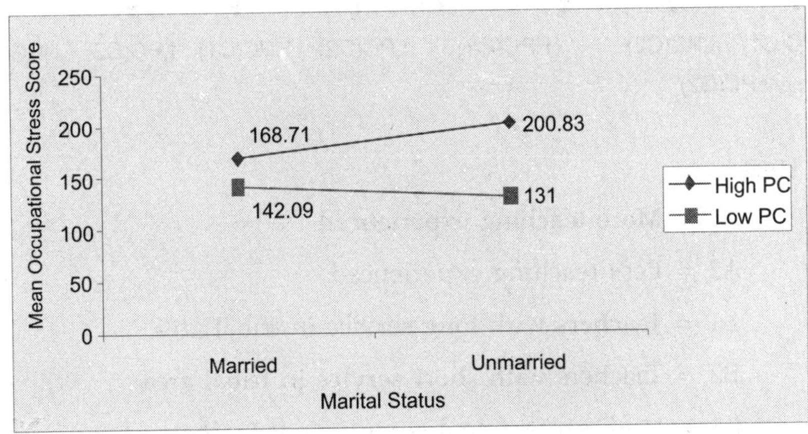

Fig. 5.2(b) Marital Status × Professional Commitment Interaction for Female Teachers

SUB SECTION—II

(*a*) Mean Differences in Job Satisfaction in Relation to Professional Commitment, Service in Tribal Area and Teaching Experience

Here, two categories of professional commitment i.e. high professional commitment and low professional commitment; teaching experience i.e. more teaching experience and less teaching experience, two levels of service in tribal area i.e. long service in tribal area and short service in tribal area were taken up. So, a 2 × 2 × 2 factorial design was prepared as follows:

Factorial Design

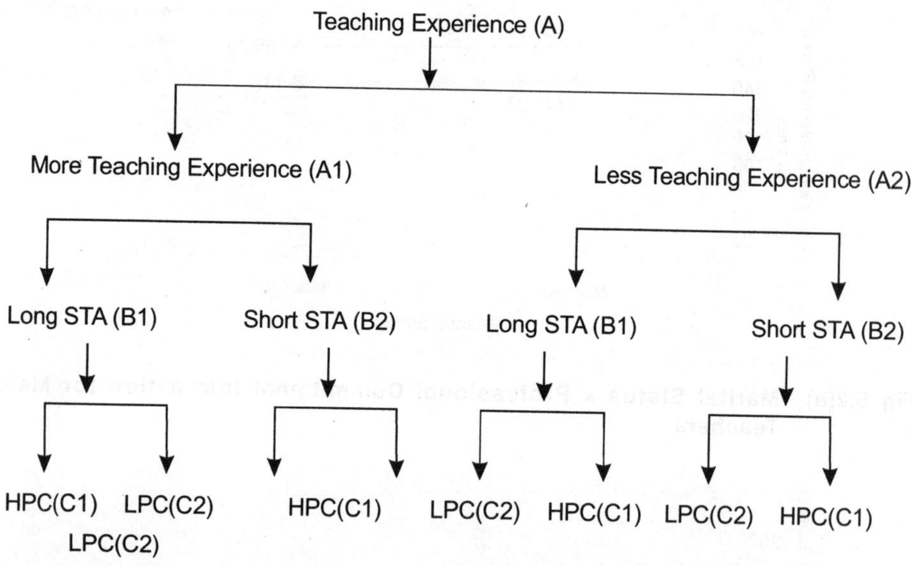

Here,

A1 = More teaching experienced

A2 = Less teaching experienced

B1 = Teachers with long service in tribal area

B2 = Teachers with short service in tribal area

C1 = High professional commitment teachers

C2 = Low professional commitment teachers

Table 5.8 : Mean Job Satisfaction Scores in relation to category of Professional Commitment, Service in tribal area and Teaching Experience

Groups	More Teaching Experience		Less Teaching Experience	
	Long STA	Short STA	Long STA	Short STA
High P.C.	173.85	178.90	145.14	188.27
Low P.C.	160.89	145.76	161.25	160.77

Mean score of teaches with long service in tribal area = 162.96
Mean scores of teachers with short service in tribal area = 171.50
Mean scores of high professional committed teachers = 176.95
Mean scores of low professional committed teachers = 158.79

Table 5.9 : Summary showing Analysis of Variance on Job-Satisfaction scores in relation to Professional Commitment, Service in Tribal Areas and Teaching Experience (N=236)

Sources of Variation	Df	SS	MS	F-ratio	Level of significance
Teaching Experience (A)	1	808.81	808.01	1.25	n.s.
STA(B)	1	4278.57	4278.57	6.61	P < .05
Professional Commitment (C)	1	19436.03	19436.00	30.02	P < .01
AxB	1	5720.74	5720.74	8.84	P < .05
BxC	1	372.36	372.36	0.57	n.s.
AxC	1	14.54	14.54	0.02	n.s.
AxBxC	1	12490.03	12490.03	19.29	P < .01
Error	228	147594.82	647.35		-

n.s. Indicates not significant at 0.05 levels.

INTERPRETATION

Main Effects

(1) Table 5.9 shows that F-ratio for the main effect of category of teaching experience (A) at 1/228 df is less than the table value at 0.05 level of significance. It means that there exists no significant difference in job-satisfaction of more teaching experience and less teaching experience teachers. Thus, the hypothesis of significant difference in job-satisfaction of more and less teaching experienced teachers is not accepted.

(2) F-ratio for the main effect of service in tribal area (B) at 1/228 df is more than the table value at 0.05 level of significance. It means that there exists a significant difference in job-satisfaction of long and short service in tribal area of teachers. Thus, the hypothesis of significant differences in job satisfaction of long and short service in tribal area of teachers is accepted.

Further, the mean scores of long service in tribal area exhibit less job-satisfaction (M=162.96) than short service in tribal area (M=171.50). Hence, service in tribal area as a single main variable shows significant effect on job-satisfaction.

(3) F-ratio for the main effect of professional commitment of teachers (C) at 1/228 df is more than the table value of 0.01 level of significance. It means that there sexists significant difference in job satisfaction of high and low professional commitment. Thus, the hypothesis of significant difference in job-satisfaction of high and low professional commitment is accepted.

Further, the mean value shows the high professional commitment teachers exhibit more job satisfaction (M=176.95) than low professional commitment teachers (M=158.79). Hence, professional commitment as a single main variable shows significant effect on job satisfaction.

Interactional Effects

(4) The calculated F-ratio for the two factor interaction of category of teaching experience and service in tribal area (A × B) is more than the table value at 0.01 level of significance. It means the difference between the mean job-satisfaction scores of more teaching experienced teachers with long and short service in tribal area is significantly different from the mean job-satisfaction scores of less teaching experienced teachers with long and short service in tribal area. Thus, the hypothesis of significant interaction between category of teaching experience and service in tribal area of teachers on job-satisfaction is accepted. The significant interaction is depicted in Fig. 5.3 (*See on next page*)

(5) The calculated F-ratio for the two factor interaction of category of service in tribal area and professional commitment (B × C) is less than the table value at 0.05 level of significance. This shows that the differences between the mean job-satisfaction scores of high professional commitment teachers whether long or short service an tribal area is not significantly different from the mean job-satisfaction scores of low professional commitment teacher whether long or short

service in tribal area. Thus, the hypothesis of significant interaction between professional commitment and service in tribal area of teachers on their job- satisfaction is not accepted.

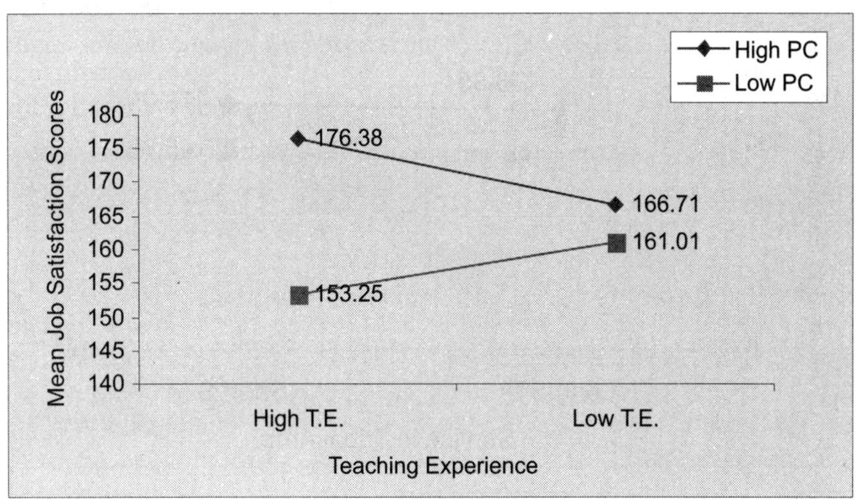

Fig. 5.3 : Teaching Experience × Professional Commitment Interaction

(6) The calculated F-ratio for the two-factor interaction of category of professional commitment and teaching experience (A × C) is less than the table value at .05 levels of significance. This shows that the difference between the mean job-satisfaction scores of high professional commitment teachers whether more or less teaching experience is not significantly different from the mean job-satisfaction scores of low professional commitment teachers whether more or less teaching experience. Hence, the hypothesis of significant interaction between professional commitment and teaching experience of teachers on job-satisfaction is not accepted.

(7) The calculated F-ratio for the three factors interaction of category of teaching experience, service in tribal area and professional commitment of teachers (A × B × C) is more than the table value at 0.01 level of significance. So, the interactive effect of three variables on job-satisfaction of teachers is significant. This indicates that category of teaching experience, service in tribal area and professional commitment of teachers together reveal significant difference on teachers' job-satisfaction. Hence, the hypothesis of significant triple interaction between category of teaching experience, service in tribal area and professional commitment of teachers on job satisfaction is accepted. The same has been depicted graphically in Fig. 5.4.

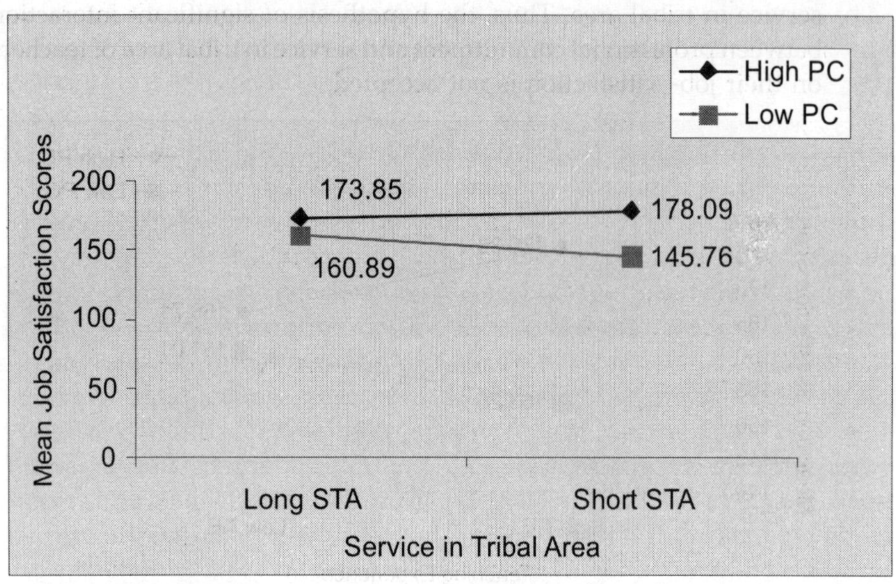

Fig. 5.4(a) Service in Tribal Area × Professional Commitment Interaction for More Teaching Experience Teachers

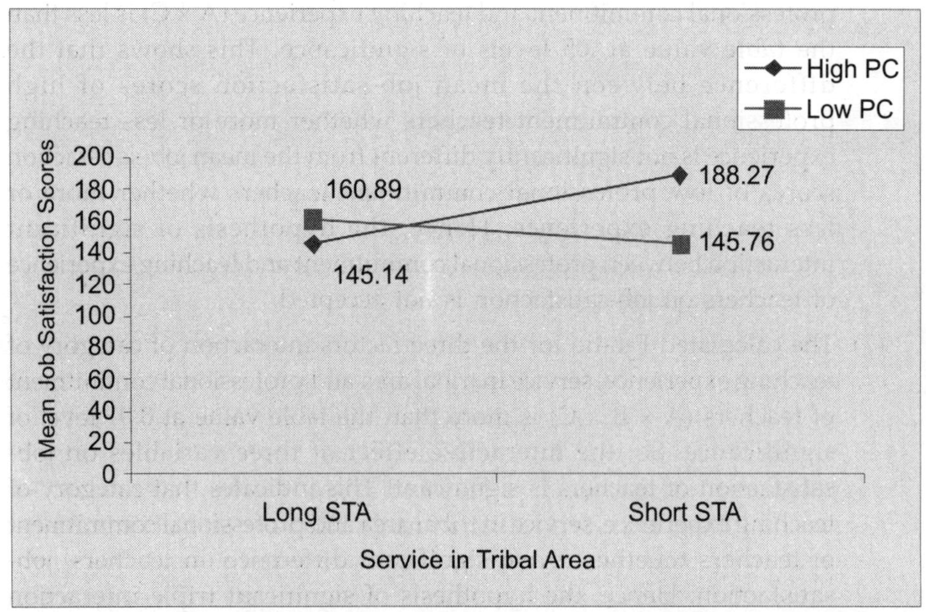

Fig. 5.4(b) Service in Tribal Area × Professional Commitment Interaction for Less Teaching Experience Teachers

(*b*) Mean Differences in Occupational Stress in Relation to Professional Commitment, Service in Tribal Area and Teaching Experience

Table 5.10 : Mean Occupational Stress Scores of Teachers in relation to category of Professional Commitment, Service in Tribal Area and Teaching Experience

Groups	More Teaching Experience		Less Teaching Experience	
	Long STA	Short STA	Long STA	Short STA
High P.C.	M1 = 168.00	M2 =168.71	M3 =135.64	M4 =182.27
Low P.C.	M5 =141.91	M6 =134.06	M7 =145.75	M8 =150.48

Mean score of long service teachers in tribal area = 149.81
Mean score of short service teachers in tribal area = 162.56
Mean score of more teaching experience teachers = 153.16
Mean score of less teaching experience teachers = 160.12
Mean Score of high professional commitment teachers = 169.79
Mean score of low professional commitment teachers = 144.41

Table 5.11 : Summary showing Analysis of Variance on Occupational Stress of Teachers in relation to Professional Commitment, Service in Tribal Area and Teaching Experience (N=236)

Sources of Variation	Df	SS	MS	F-ratio	Level of significance
Teaching Experience (A)	1	37959.76	37959.76	132.79	P < .01
STA(B)	1	2853.95	2853.95	9.98	P < .01
Professional Commitment (C)	1	957.96	9537.96	33.37	P < .01
AxB	1	5108.61	5108.61	17.87	P < .01
BxC	1	5.59	5.59	0.02	n.s.
AxC	1	280.42	280.42	0.98	n.s.
AxBxC	1	9427.07	9427.07	32.98	P < .01
Error	228	65173.36	285.85		-

n.s. Indicates not significant at 0.05 levels.

INTERPRETATION

Main Effects

(1) F-ratio for the main effect of teaching experience of the teacher (A) at 1/228 df is more than the table value at 0.01 level of significance. It

means that there exists significant difference in occupational stress of more teaching experience and less teaching experience of teachers. Thus, the hypothesis of significant difference in occupational stress of high and low teaching experience of teachers is accepted.

Further, the mean values show that teacher with more teaching experience exhibit less occupational stress (M=153.16) than teachers of less teaching experience (M=160.12) Hence, teaching of experience as a single main variable shows significant effect on occupational stress.

(2) F-ratio for the main effect of service in tribal area of the teacher (B) at 1/228 df is more than the table value at 0.01 level of significance. It means that there exists significant difference in occupational stress of long and short service in tribal area of teachers. Thus, the hypothesis of significant difference in occupational stress of long and short service in tribal area is accepted.

Further, the mean values show that the teachers of long service in tribal area exhibit less occupational stress (M=149.81) than the teachers of short service in tribal area (M=162.56). Hence service is tribal area (STA) as a single main variable shows significant effect on occupational stress.

(3) F-ratio for the main effect of professional commitment (C) of teachers at 1/228 is more than the table value at 0.01 levels of significance. It means that there exists significant difference in occupational stress of high and low professional commitment of teachers. Thus, the hypothesis of significant difference in occupational stress is accepted.

Further, the mean values show that the teachers of high professional commitment exhibit more occupational stress (M=169.79) than the teachers of low professional commitment (M=144.41). Hence, professional commitment as a single main variable shows significant effect on occupational stress.

Interactional Effects

(4) The calculated F-ratio for the two-factor interaction of category of teaching experience and service in tribal area (A × B) is more than the table value at 0.01 levels of significance. This shows that the difference between the mean occupational stress scores of more teaching experience teachers whether long or short service in tribal area is significantly different from the mean occupational stress scores of less teaching experience whether long or short service in tribal area. Thus, the hypothesis of significant interaction between

category of teaching experience and service in tribal area of teachers on occupational stress is accepted. The significant interaction is depicted in Fig. 5.5.

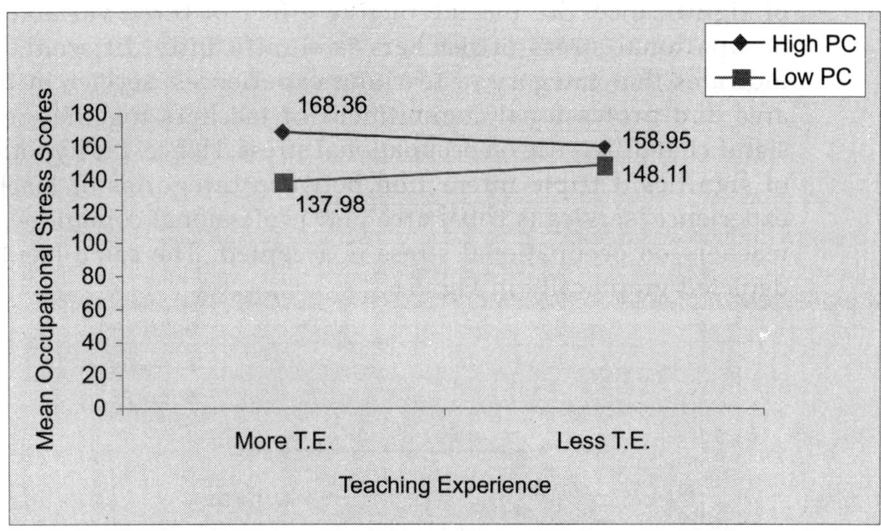

Fig. 5.5 : Teaching Experience × Professional Commitment

(5) The calculated F-ratio for the two factor professional commitment and service in tribal area (B × C) is less than the table value at 0.05 levels of significance. This shows that, the difference between the mean occupational stress scores of high professional commitment teachers whether long or short service in tribal area is not significantly different from the mean occupational stress scores of low professional committed teachers whether long or short service in tribal area. Thus, the hypothesis of significant interaction between category of professional commitment and service in tribal area of teacher on occupational stress is not accepted.

(6) The calculated F-ratio for the two factor teaching experience and professional commitment (A × C) is less than the table value at 0.05 levels of significance. This shows that the difference between the mean occupational stress scores of high professional committed teachers whether more or less teaching experience is not significantly different from the mean occupational stress scores of low professional committed teachers whether more or less teaching experience. Thus, the hypothesis of significant interaction between category of teaching experience and professional commitment of teachers on occupational stress is not accepted.

(7) The calculated F-ratio for three factor interaction of category of teaching experience, service in tribal area and professional commitment (A × B × C) is more than the table value at 0.01 level of significance. So, the interactive effect of three variables on occupational stress of teachers is significantly different. This indicates that category of teaching experiences, service in tribal area and professional commitment of teachers together reveal significant difference on occupational stress. Hence, the hypothesis of significant triple interaction between categories of teaching experience, service is tribal area and professional commitment of teachers on occupational stress is accepted. The same has been depicted graphically in Fig. 5.6.

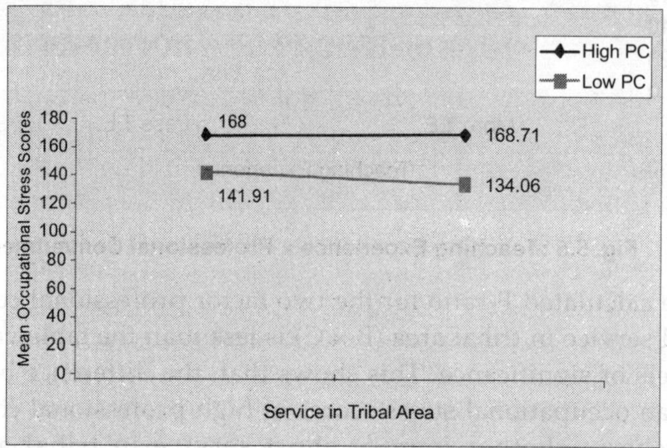

Fig. 5.6(a) Service in Tribal Area × Professional Commitment Interaction for More Teaching Experience Teachers

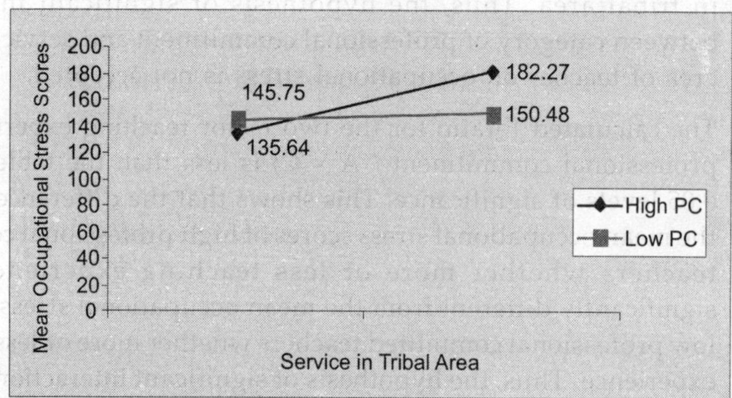

Fig. 5.6(b) Service in Tribal Area × Professional Commitment Interaction for Less Teaching Experience Teachers

SUB-SECTION—III

(a) Mean Differences in Job-satisfaction in Relation to Professional Commitment, Socio-economic Status and Family Size

The investigator dealt with the study of mean differences in job-satisfaction with respect to category of professional commitment, socio-economic status and family size. For this purpose, the investigator applied three-way analysis of variance technique. Here, two levels of professional commitment i.e. high professional commitment and low professional commitment; three categories of socio-economic status i.e. high socio-economic status, middle socio-economic status, low socio-economic status and two levels of family size, i.e. large family size and small family size. So, 3 × 2 × 2 factorial design was prepared as follows:

Factorial Design

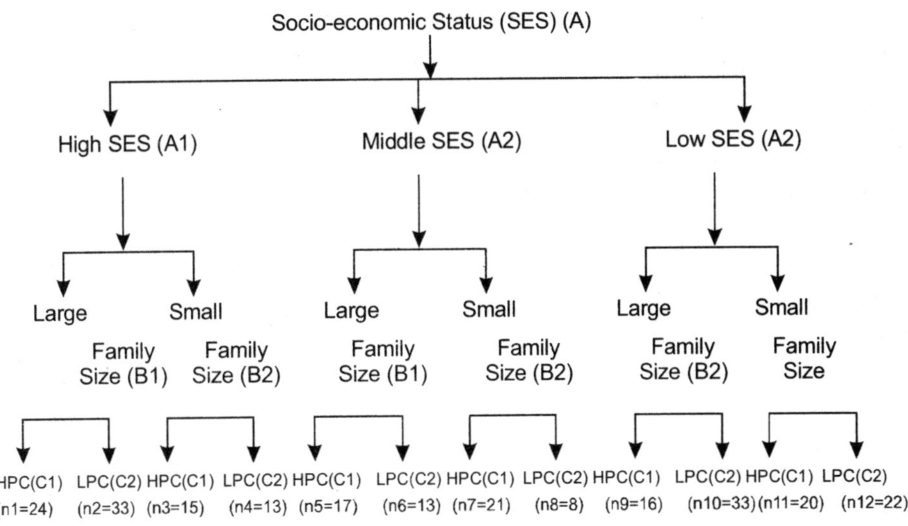

Here,

A1 = High socio-economic status teachers.

A2 = Middle socio-economic status teachers.

A3 = Low socio-economic status teachers.

B1 = Large family size teachers.

B2 = Small family size teachers.

C1 = High professional commitment teachers.

C2 = Low professional commitment teachers.

The summary of job satisfaction scores in various cells of factorial design followed by summary of ANOVA result are given in below table 5.12 and 5.13.

Table 5.12 : Mean Job Satisfaction scores in relation to category of Professional Commitment, Socio-economic Status and Family Size

Groups	Large Family Size		Small Family Size	
	HPC	LPC	HPC	LPC
HSES	M1=177.96	M2 =152.64	M3 =186.93	M4 =153.85
MSES	M5 =175.12	M6 =157.77	M7 =177.52	M8 =148.37
LSES	M9 =171.56	M10=153.33	M11 =170.60	M12 =147.00

Mean score of high professional commitment teachers = 177.32
Mean scores of low professional commitment teachers = 159.48

Table 5.13 : Summary of ANOVA on Job-satisfaction of teachers in relation to Professional Commitment, Socio-economic Status and Family Size (N=236)

Sources of Variation	Df	SS	MS	F-ratio	Level of signifi-cance
SES (A)	2	104.90	52.45	0.97	n.s.
Family size (B)	1	1.41	1.41	0.03	n.s.
Professional Commitment (C)	1	1794.14	1794.14	33.05	p<0.01
AxB	2	50.03	25.015	0.46	n.s.
BxC	2	36.50	18.25	0.08	n.s.
AxC	1	4.32	4.32	0.34	n.s.
AxBxC	2	52.76	26.38	0.49	n.s.
Error	224	12159.23	54.28	—	—

n.s. Indicates not significant at 0.05 levels.

INTERPRETATION

Main Effects

(1) F-ratio for the main effect of socio-economic status (A) of the teachers at 2/224 df is less than the table value at 0.05 level of significance. It means that there is no significant difference in job-satisfaction of high, middle and low socio-economic status of teachers. Hence, the hypothesis of significant difference in job-satisfaction of teachers belong to different socio-economic status is not accepted.

(2) F-ratio for the main effect of family Size (B) of the teachers at 1/224 df is less than the table value at 0.05 level of significance. It means that there exists no significant difference in job satisfaction of large and small family size teachers. Hence, the hypothesis of significant difference in job satisfaction of teachers of different category of family size is not accepted.

(3) F-ratio for the main effect of professional commitment (C) at 1/224 df is more than the table value at 0.01 level of significance. It means that there exists significant difference in job-satisfaction of high and low professional commitment teachers. Thus, the hypothesis of significant difference in job-satisfaction of professional commitment is accepted.

Further, the mean scores of high professional commitment teacher have high job-satisfaction (M=177.32) than the teachers of low professional commitment (M=159.48). Therefore, professional commitment as a single main variable shows significant effect on job satisfaction.

Interaction Effects

(4) The calculated F-ratio for the two factors interaction of category socio-economic status and family size (A × B) is less than the table value at 0.05 levels of significance. So, there is significant difference between mean job-satisfaction scores of high, low and middle socio-economic status teachers having large or small family size. Therefore, the hypothesis of significant difference in interaction of category socio-economic status and family size is not accepted.

(5) The calculated F-ratio for the two-factor interaction of category of family size and professional commitment (B x C) is less than the table value at 0.05 level of significance. Hence, there is no significant difference between mean job satisfaction scores of high and low professional commitment teachers having large and small family size. Therefore, the hypothesis of significant difference in interaction of category of family size and professional commitment is not accepted.

(6) The calculated F-ratio for the two-factor interaction of category of socio-economic status and professional commitment (A × C) is less than the table value at 0.05 levels of significance. So, there exits no significant difference between mean job- satisfaction scores of high, middle and low socio-economic status teachers having high or low professional commitment. The hypothesis of significant difference in interaction of category of socio-economic status and professional commitment is not accepted.

(7) The calculated F-ratio for the triple interaction of category of professional commitment, socio- economic status and family size (A × B × C) is less than the table value at 0.05 levels of significance. So, there is no significant interactional effect of category of professional commitment, socio-economic status and family size on job satisfaction. This indicates that category of professional commitment; socio-economic status and family size of teachers together reveal insignificant difference on job-satisfaction. The hypothesis of significant interactional effect between category of professional commitment, socio-economic status and family size on job-satisfaction is not accepted.

(b) Mean Differences in Occupational Stress in Relation to Professional Commitment, Socio-economic Status and Family Size

Table 5.14 : Mean Occupational Stress scores in relation to category of Professional Commitment, Socio-economic Status and Family Size

Groups	Large Family Size		Small Family Size	
	HPC	LPC	HPC	LPC
HSES	M1=173.17	M2=141.57	M3=177.33	M4=141.38
MSES	M5=168.71	M6=136.61	M7=173.29	M8=137.50
LSES	M9=158.81	M10=149.06	M11=162.30	M12=138.52

Mean score of high professional commitment teachers = 169.11
Mean scores of low professional commitment teachers = 142.20

Table 5.15 : Summary showing ANOVA on Occupational Stress of Teachers in relation to Professional Commitment, Socio-economic Status and Family size (N=236)

Sources of Variation	Df	SS	MS	F-ratio	Level of significance
SES (A)	2	80.74	40.37	1.12	n.s.
Family Size (B)	1	0.48	0.48	0.01	n.s.
Professional Commitment (C)	1	2379.24	2379.24	65.96	p<0.01
AxB	2	23.36	11.68	0.32	n.s.
BxC	1	3.38	3.38	0.09	n.s.
AxC	2	194.66	97.33	2.70	n.s.
AxBxC	2	54.15	27.075	0.75	n.s.
Error	224	8079.48	36.07	-	-

n.s. Indicates not significant at 0.05 levels.

INTERPRETATION

Main effects

(1) F-ratio for the main effect of socio-economic status (A) of the teachers at 2/224 df is less than the table value at 0.05 level of significance. It means that there exists no significant difference between in occupational stress of high socio-economic status, middle socio-economic status and low socio-economic status teachers. Hence, the hypothesis of significant difference in teachers belonging to different socio-economic status is not accepted.

(2) F-ratio for the main effect of family size (B) of teachers at 1/224 df is less than the table value at 0.05 level of significance. It means that there exists no significant difference in occupational stress of large family size and small family size. So, the hypothesis of significant difference in occupational stress of large family size and small family of teachers is not accepted.

(3) F-ratio for the main effect of professional commitment (C) of the teacher at 1/224 df is more than the table value at 0.01 level of significance on occupational stress. It means that there exists significant difference in occupational stress of high professional commitment and low professional commitment teachers. Thus, hypothesis of significant difference of professional commitment on occupational stress is accepted.

Further, the mean values show that teachers of high professional commitment exhibit high occupational stress (M=169.11) than the teachers of low professional commitment (M=142.20). Hence, professional commitment as a single main variable shows significant effect on occupational stress.

Interaction Effects

(4) The calculated F-ratio for the two-factor interaction of category of socio-economic status and size of the family (A × B) is less than the table value at 0.05 levels of significance. This shows that the difference between the mean occupational stress scores of high, middle and low socio-economic status teachers having more and less numbers of dependants (family size) is not significant. The hypothesis of significant interaction between category of SES and size of the family is not accepted.

(5) The calculated F-ratio for the two-factor interaction or category of family size and professional commitment (B × C) is less than the table value at 0.05 levels of significance. This shows that there is no

difference between the mean occupational stress scores of high and low professional commitment teacher's whether large or small family size. Therefore, the hypothesis of significant interaction between category of family size and professional commitment is not accepted.

(6) The calculated F-ratio for the two-factor interaction of category of professional commitment and socio-economic status (A × C) is less than the table value at 0.05 level of significant. This shows that the difference between the mean occupational stress scores of high and low professional commitment teachers having different level of socio-economic status is not significant. So, the hypothesis of significant interaction between category of socio-economic status and professional commitment is not accepted.

(7) The calculated F-ratio for the three-factor interaction of category of professional commitment, socio-economic status and family size (A x B × C) is less than the table value of 0.05 levels of significance. So, the interactive effect of three variables on occupational stress of teachers is not significantly different. This indicates the category of socio-economic status; family size and professional commitment of teachers together reveal insignificant difference on occupational stress. So, the hypothesis of significant triple interaction between category of professional commitment, socio-economic status and family size of teachers on occupational stress is not accepted.

SECTION—C

Inter-Correlation between Job-satisfaction, Occupation Stress and Professional Commitment

Section—C is divided into four sub-sections. They are described in detail below:

Sub-section—I

This sub-section deals with correlation of eight dimensions of job-satisfaction with twelve dimensions of occupational stress (*See Table 5.16 on next page*).

Different dimensions of job satisfaction and occupational stress are given below:

Dimensions of Job-satisfaction Scale

1. Intrinsic aspect of the job
2. Salary, promotional avenues and service conditions
3. Physical facilities
4. Institutional plans and policies

Table 5.16 : Inter-correlation Matrix of Job Satisfaction with Occupational Stress

	Job Satisfaction Dimension						Occupation Stress Dimensions					
	1	2	3	4	5	6	7	8	9	10	11	12
1.	0.24**	0.35**	0.31**	0.19*	0.06	0.37**	0.40**	0.33**	0.51**	0.27**	0.44**	0.15*
2.	0.29**	0.13*	0.98**	0.22**	0.25**	0.03	0.15*	0.15*	0.21**	0.23**	0.24**	0.30**
3.	0.20**	0.20**	0.18*	0.18*	0.08	0.20**	0.06	0.25**	0.43**	0.27**	0.32**	0.17*
4.	0.29**	0.46**	0.48**	0.40**	0.16*	0.39**	0.31**	0.41**	0.58**	0.42**	0.56**	0.20**
5.	0.34**	0.27**	0.37**	0.26**	0.004	0.30**	0.35**	0.28**	0.37**	0.35**	0.47**	0.09
6.	0.22**	0.27**	0.33**	0.15*	-0.03	0.23**	0.24**	0.26**	0.43**	0.27**	0.41**	0.12*
7.	0.32**	0.42**	0.49**	0.38**	0.01	0.39**	0.39**	0.48**	0.52**	0.44**	0.57**	0.26**
8.	0.28**	0.34**	0.42**	0.32**	-0.02	0.33**	0.35**	0.29**	0.45**	0.34**	0.49**	0.08

* Significant at 0.05 level
** Significant at 0.01 levels

5. Satisfaction with authorities
6. Satisfaction with social status and family welfare
7. Rapport with students
8. Relationship with co-workers

Dimensions of Occupational Stress

1. Role overload
2. Role ambiguity
3. Role conflict
4. Unreasonable group and political pressure
5. Responsibility for persons
6. Under participation
7. Powerlessness
8. Poor peer relations
9. Intrinsic impoverishment
10. Low status
11. Strenuous working conditions
12. Un-profitability

INTERPRETATION

(1) Table 5.16 indicates correlation coefficients between intrinsic aspect of the job satisfaction with role overload, role ambiguity, role conflict, under participation, powerlessness, poor peer relations, low status dimensions of occupational stress are 0.24, 0.35, 0.31, 0.37, 0.40, 0.33, and 0.27 respectively. These correlation coefficients are positive and low. However, they are significant at 0.01 levels. It shows that there exist positive, low but significant relationship between intrinsic aspect of the job and with role overload, role ambiguity, role-conflict, under participation, powerlessness, poor peer relations and low status dimensions of occupational stress. Further, there exists positive, negligible but significant correlation between intrinsic aspect of the job with unreasonable group and political pressures and un-profitability dimensions of occupational stress having coefficients of 0.19, 0.15 respectively. Moreover, whereas intrinsic aspect of the job has positive, average but significant correlation with intrinsic impoverishment and strenuous working conditions dimensions of

occupational stress having coefficient 0.51, 0.44 respectively; coefficient of correlation between intrinsic aspects of the job with responsibility for persons is 0.06, which is positive, negligible and insignificant.

(2) Co-efficient of correlation between salary, promotional avenues and service conditions dimensions of job-satisfaction with role conflict dimension of occupational stress is positive and very high (r = 0.98) as well as significant at 0.01 level. It shows that there exists positive, very high and significant relationship. On the other hand, whereas salary, promotional avenues and service conditions dimension of job satisfaction have positive, low but significant correlation with role overload, unreasonable group and political pressure, responsibility for persons, intrinsic impoverishment, low status, strenuous working conditions and un-profitability dimensions of occupational stress 0.5 (r=0.29, 0.22, 0.25, 0.21, 0.23, 0.24, 0.30 respectively), but it has positive, negligible but significant correlation with role ambiguity, powerlessness, and poor peer relations (0.13, 0.15, 0.15 respectively) dimensions of occupational stress.

(3) Physical facilities dimensions of job has average, positive but significant correlation with intrinsic impoverishment dimension of occupational stress having co-efficient 0.43. Further, physical facilities has low, positive but significant relation with poor peer relations, low status, strenuous working dimensions of occupational stress at 0.25, 0.27 0.32 coefficient respectively but physical facilities have positive, negligible but significant correlation with role overload, role ambiguity, role conflict unreasonable group and political pressure, under participation, un-profitability, dimensions of occupational stress having co-efficients 0.20, 0.20, 0.18, 0.18, 0.20 respectively. Moreover, physical facilities have coefficient of correlation with responsibility for person and powerlessness as 0.08, 0.06 respectively, which are positive, very negligible but insignificant.

(4) Co-efficient of correlation between institutional plans and policies dimension of job-satisfaction with role ambiguity, role conflict, unreasonable group and political pressure, poor peer relations, intrinsic impoverishment, low status, strenuous working condition dimensions of occupational stress are 0.46, 0.48, 0.40, 0.41, 0.58, 0.42, 0.56 respectively, which are positive, average and significant. Further, institutional plans and policies have co-efficients of 0.29, 0.39, and 0.31 with role overload, under participation, powerlessness dimensions of occupational stress respectively. These co-efficients show positive, low but significant correlation. However, there is positive, negligible but significant correlation between institutional

plans and policies with responsibility for persons and un-profitability dimensions of occupational stress having co-efficients 0.16, 0.20 respectively.

(5) The co-efficient of correlation between satisfaction with authorities and strenuous working condition is 0.47. From this it is clear that there is positive, average but significant correlation between satisfaction with authorities and strenuous working conditions. The co-efficient of correlations of satisfaction with authorities with role overload, role ambiguity, role conflict, unreasonable group and political pressures, under participation, powerlessness, poor peer relations and interinsic impoverishment and low status dimensions of occupational stress are 0.34, 0.27, 0.37, 0.26, 0.30, 0.35, 0.28, 0.37 and 0.35 respectively. These co-efficients indicate there is positive, low but significant correlation between satisfaction with authorities and role overload, role ambiguity, role conflict, unreasonable group and political pressure, under participation, powerlessness, poor peer relation, interinsic impoverishment and low status dimensions of occupational stress. Further, satisfaction with authority dimension of job satisfaction has coefficient correlation of 0.004, 0.09 with responsibility for persons, unprofitability dimensions of occupational stress respectively. These co-efficients indicate that satisfaction with authorities has positive negligible but insignificant correlation with responsibility for persons and un-profitability dimensions of occupational stress.

(6) Satisfaction with social status and family welfare dimension of job satisfaction has coefficients of correlation 0.15 and 0.12 with unreasonable group and political pressure, un-profitability dimensions of occupational stress respectively. These co-efficients indicate positive, negligible but significant correlation. The co-efficients of correlation of satisfaction with social status and family welfare with role overload, role ambiguity, role conflict, under participation, powerlessness, poor peer relations and low status dimensions of occupational stress are 0.22, 0.27, 0.33, 0.24, 0.24, 0.26, 0.27 respectively. So there is positive low but significant correlation between them. Satisfaction with authorities has positive, average but significant correlation with interinsic impoverishment, strenuous working condition dimensions of occupational stress having coefficients of correlation 0.43, 0.41 respectively.

(7) Coefficients of correlation of rapport with student's dimension of job-satisfaction with role ambiguity, role conflict, poor peer relations, interinsic impoverishment, low status and strenuous

working condition dimensions of occupational stress are 0.42, 0.49, 0.48, 0.52, 0.44 and 0.57 respectively. These co-efficients of correlation show positive, average but significant correlation. Besides, rapport with students has positive low but significant correlation with role overload, unreasonable group and political pressure, under participation, powerlessness and un-profitability dimensions of occupational stress having coefficient of correlations are 0.32, 0.38, 0.39, 0.39, 0.26 respectively. However, rapport with students' dimension of job-satisfaction has positive, negligible but insignificant correlation with responsibility for persons, whose coefficient of correlation is 0.01.

(8) The coefficient of correlation between relationship with co-workers dimension of job satisfaction with role conflict, interinsic impoverishment, and strenuous working condition dimensions of occupational stress are 0.42, 0.45, and 0.49 respectively.These correlation of coefficients are positive, average but significant. Further, relationship with co-workers has positive, low but significant correlation with role overload, role ambiguity, unreasonable group political pressure, under participation, powerlessness, poor peer relations and low status dimensions of occupational stress having coefficient of correlation 0.28, 0.34, 0.32, 0.33, 0.35, 0.29 and 0.49 respectively. However, relationship with workers has only negative, negligible but insignificant correlation with responsibility for persons having co-efficient of correlation (-0.02). Moreover, relationship with co-workers has positive, very negligible but insignificant correlation with un-profitability dimensions of occupational stress having coefficient of correlation 0.08.

Sub-section—II

This sub-section describes the nature of relationship between professional commitment and with eight dimensions of job satisfaction.

Table 5.17 : Intercor relation Matrix of Professional Commitment with Dimensions of Job-Satisfaction

	Dimensions of Job Satisfaction							
	1	2	3	4	5	6	7	8
Professional Commitment	0.23**	-0.01	0.08	0.25**	0.26**	0.26**	0.32**	0.18

*Significant at 0.05 level
**Significant at 0.01 levels.

INTERPRETATION

Table 5.17 indicates the coefficient of correlations between professional commitment with interinsic aspect of the job, institutional plans and policies, satisfaction with authorities, satisfaction with social status and family welfare, rapport with students dimensions of job satisfaction are 0.23, 0.25, 0.26, 0.26, and 0.32 respectively. These correlations of co-efficient indicate that there exists positive, low but significant correlation between these factors.

Whereas, professional commitment has negative, negligible but insignificant correlation with role ambiguity (r = –0.01). Yet professional commitment has positive, negligible but significant correlation with relationship with co-workers whose coefficient of correlation is 0.18.

Sub-section III

This sub-section delineates the correlation between professional commitment and twelve dimensions of occupational stress.

Table 5.18 : Inter correlation Matrix of Professional Commitment with dimensions of Occupational Stress

	Dimensions of occupational stress											
	1	2	3	4	5	6	7	8	9	10	11	12
Profess-Ional Commit-ment	0.38**	0.37**	0.38**	0.22**	0.16*	0.42**	0.35**	0.35**	0.39**	0.39**	0.36**	0.19*

* Significant at 0.05 level
** Significant at 0.01 level

INTERPRETATION

Only professional commitment has positive, average and significant correlation with under participation dimension of occupational stress whose co-efficient of correlation is 0.42. Professional commitment has positive, negligible but significant correlation with responsibility for persons, un-profitability dimensions of occupational stress having co-efficient of correlations 0.16 and 0.19 respectively. The co-efficient of correlations of professional commitment with role overload, role ambiguity, role conflict, unreasonable group and political pressure, powerlessness, poor peer relations, interinsic impoverishment, low status, and strenuous working condition, dimensions of occupational stress are 0.38, 0.37, 0.38, 0.22, 0.35, 0.35, 0.39, 0.39 and 0.36 respectively. So these co-efficient of correlations exhibit, positive, low but significant correlation.

Sub-section—IV

This sub section describes correlation of professional commitment with job satisfaction and occupational stress as a whole.

Table 5.19 : Inter Correlation Matrix of Professional Commitment with Job Satisfaction and Occupational Stress

	Professional commitment	Occupational stress	Job satisfaction
Professional commitment	1.0	.27**	.42**
Occupational stress	—	1.0	.51**
Job satisfaction	—	—	1.0

** Significant at 0.01 level.

INTERPRETATION

Co-efficient of correlation between professional commitment and occupational stress is .27, which is positive, low but significant at 0.01 levels. It shows that there exists a significant positive relationship between professional commitment and occupational stress. The hypothesis of significant, positive correlation between occupational stress and professional commitment is accepted. This explains that if teachers are committed to their profession, a number of stressful situations will come before them. If teachers are not committed, they will not face any stress.

Co-efficient of correlation between professional commitment and job satisfaction is .42, which is positive, average but significant at 0.01 levels. It shows that there exists positive significant relationship between professional commitment and job satisfaction. The hypothesis of significant, positive connection between professional commitment and job-satisfaction is accepted. This indicates that those teachers are committed to their profession; they are also satisfied with their job.

Co-efficient of correlation between job satisfaction and occupational stress is 0.51, which is positive, average but significant at 0.01 levels. So, there exists a significant difference between job-satisfaction and occupational stress of primary school teacher in tribal area. The hypothesis of significant relationship between job satisfaction and occupational stress is accepted. It is inferred that occupational stress has effect on job-satisfaction.

6

Main Findings and Educational Implications

After analysis and interpretation of the data, the next step is presentation of the main findings, discussion of the results and most important of all the educational implications of the results. In the end, suggestions for further research are also given.

Main Findings

Main findings of the study are given in the following sections in the light of the interpretation of the results.

SECTION-A : FINDINGS BASED ON LEVEL OF PROFESSIONAL COMMITMENT, JOB SATISFACTION AND OCCUPATIONAL STRESS

(1) From the mean scores, it is inferred that primary school teachers in tribal area have average level of job-satisfaction, moderate to high level of occupational stress and are highly committed to their profession.

Discussion

From the findings, teachers in tribal area have high professional commitment but experience moderate to high level of occupational stress and average degree of job-satisfaction. Due to high commitment to the profession, teachers discharge their service at the expense of own resource, money and leisure even after facing moderate to high level of occupational stress depending upon their place of work and uncongenial conditions in tribal area. These findings are directly or indirectly supported by Gaur & Dhaman (2003).

SECTION-B : FINDINGS BASED ON ANALYSIS OF VARIANCE

(A) Mean scores of job satisfaction of teachers were used to compute the differences in relation to professional commitment, sex and marital status.

It has been found that:

(2) There exists a significant difference between high and low professional commitment teachers on job-satisfaction. The mean scores indicate that high professionally committed teachers exhibit high job-satisfaction as compared to low professionally committed teachers.

(3) There is significant three-factor interaction of sex, marital status and professional commitment on teacher's job-satisfaction.

(4) Other main effects such as sex and marital status and interactional effect i.e. sex and marital status, sex and professional commitment, marital and professional commitment do not exhibit significant difference on job-satisfaction of teachers.

(B) Mean scores of occupational stress of teachers were used to compute the differences in it in relation to professional commitment, sex and marital status.

The results reveal that:

(5) There is significant difference in occupational stress of high and low professional commitment teachers. The mean values show that high professional committed teachers have high occupational stress as compared to low professionally committed teachers.

(6) There exists significant difference in occupational stress of three factors interactional effect of sex, marital status and professional commitment of teachers.

(7) Other main effects such as sex and marital status and interactional effects i.e. sex and professional commitment, marital status and sex, marital status and professional commitment do not exhibit significant difference on occupational stress of teachers.

(C) Mean scores of job satisfaction of teachers were used to compute the difference in it in relation to professional commitment, teaching experience and service in tribal area.

The results reveal that:

(8) There is significant difference in job satisfaction between teachers of long service in tribal area and short service in tribal area. The mean

values indicate that those teachers who serve for a long time in tribal area have low job satisfaction than the teachers serving for a short period of time.

(9) There exists significant difference in job satisfaction of teachers belonging to high and low professional commitment. The mean scores reflect that high professionally committed teachers have more job satisfaction as compared to low professionally committed teachers.

(10) There is significant difference in job satisfaction of teaches in three-factor interaction i.e. teaching experience, service in tribal area and professional commitment.

(11) Other main effect such as teaching experience and interactional effects i.e. teaching experience and professional commitment, service in tribal area and professional commitment, teaching experience and service in tribal area do not exhibit significant difference on job-satisfaction of teachers.

(D) Mean differences in occupational stress in relation to professional commitment, teaching experience and service in tribal area.

The results indicate that:

(12) There is significant difference in occupational stress of teachers having more teaching experience and less teaching experience. The mean values show that teachers of more teaching experience exhibit less occupational stress as compared to the teachers of less teaching experience.

(13) Teachers those who are serving in tribal area show significant effect on occupational stress. The mean scores of occupational stress reveal that the teachers of long service in tribal area experience less occupational stress as compared to the teachers of short service in tribal area.

(14) There is significant two-factor interaction of teaching experience and service in tribal area on teacher's occupational stress.

(15) There exists significant three-factor interaction of teaching experience, service in tribal area and professional commitment on teachers' occupational stress.

(16) Other main effect i.e. professional commitment and interactional effects such as teaching experience and professional commitment, service in tribal area and professional commitment do not exhibit significant difference on occupational stress of teachers.

(E) Mean differences in job satisfaction of teachers in relation to professional commitment, socio-economic status and family size.

It has been found that:

(17) There exists significant difference in job-satisfaction of high and low professional commitment teachers. The mean scores reveal that high professional committed teachers have high job satisfaction as compared to the teachers of low professional commitment.

(18) Other main effects i.e. socio-economic status, family size, two factors interactional effects such as socio-economic status and professional commitment, socio-economic status and family size, professional commitment and family size; three factor interactional effect of professional commitment, family size, socio-economic status do not exhibit significant differences on job-satisfaction of teachers.

(F) Mean differences in occupational stress scores in relation to professional commitment, socio-economic status and family size.

(19) There exists significant difference in occupational stress of high and low professional commitment teachers. The mean scores reveal that high professional committed teachers exhibit high occupational stress as compared to the teachers of low professional commitment.

(20) Other main effects i.e. socio-economic status, family size, two factors interactional effects such as socio-economic status and professional commitment, socio-economic status and family size, professional commitment and family size; three factor interactional effect of professional commitment, family size, socio-economic status do not exhibit significant differences on occupational stress of teachers.

Discussion

From the findings of the present study, it is evident that there exists significant difference between teachers of high professional commitment and low professional commitment on job satisfaction. It explains that high professional commitment teachers show high job-satisfaction and low professional commitment teachers have low job satisfaction. So, professional commitment is the important indicator of job satisfaction. If a teacher is committed to his/her profession, he/she will get more satisfaction to be in the teaching profession whatever may be the situation or obstacle in it. This result is supported by the findings of Bhatt (1977).

From the findings, it is also clear that teachers who serve for a long time in tribal area have low job-satisfaction than the teachers serving for a short period of time. In tribal area, a number of avert situations come to the new comer in teaching profession. Initially, he/she may adjust with it, but in the long run, they have adverse effect on his/her working. So, teaches should not be appointed for unreasonably long period of years in tribal area. The teachers should be appointed on rotation basis. Few years' service in tribal area should be made compulsory for all teachers.

Job-satisfaction of teachers depends upon the interactional effect of sex, marital status and professional commitment.

There is no significant effect of sex, marital status of teachers on job-satisfaction. So, teachers may be male or female, married or unmarried, job-satisfaction is not affected by it. Similarly, there is also no significant effect of two-way interaction of sex and marital status on job-satisfaction. This result is supported by the findings of A.R. Annamalai (1999).

There is significant difference in occupational stress of high and low professional committed teachers. High professional committed teachers have high occupational stress than the low professional committed teachers. Those teachers who are committed to the profession face high stress in their profession. In tribal area whatever may be the situation (like local language, disinterested students, adverse physical facilities and communication difficulties etc) the committed teachers furnish their duties and responsibilities towards students, colleagues, community to enroll, retain and to bring all round development of the tribal children.

The present study reveals that more experienced teachers experience less occupational stress in tribal area than less experienced teachers. Experienced teachers become acquainted with the situations, obstacles from different sources and know how to face those situations in tribal area. So, teaching experience counts towards degree of occupational stress of a teacher.

Occupational stress depends on the interactional effect of sex, marital status and professional commitment of teachers.

Teacher having long service in tribal area experiences less occupational stress. Teachers who stay for a long time in tribal do not feel any situation stressful but rather take it lightly and handle it intelligently.

There is no significant effect of two-way interaction between sex and marital status on occupational stress. Singh, Om Parkash and Singh, Reeta (1998) support this finding.

SECTION-C : FINDING BASED ON INTER-CORRELATION

Findings based on correlation between dimensions of job-satisfaction and dimensions of occupational stress.

Main findings are as follows:

(21) Intrinsic aspect of the job satisfaction has (*i*) average, positive but significant relation with intrinsic impoverishment and strenuous working condition of occupational stress; (*ii*) has positive, low but significant relation with role overload, role ambiguity, role conflict, under participation, powerlessness, poor peer relations, and low status dimension of occupational stress; (*iii*) has positive, negligible but significant correlation with unreasonable groups and political pressure, unprofitability dimensions of occupational stress.

(22) Salary, promotional avenues and service conditions dimensions of job-satisfaction has (*i*) positive, very high and significant correlation with role conflict; (*ii*) has positive, low but significant correlation with role overload, unreasonable group and political pressure, responsibility for persons, intrinsic impoverishment, low status, strenuous working condition and unprofitability dimensions of occupational stress; (*iii*) has positive, negligible but significant correlation with role ambiguity dimension of occupational stress.

(23) Physical facilities dimensions of job-satisfaction have (*i*) positive, average and significant co-relation with intrinsic impoverishment dimension of occupational stress; (*ii*) has positive, low and significant relation with poor peer relation, low status, and strenuous working condition dimensions of occupational stress; (*iii*) has positive, negligible but significant relation with role overload, role ambiguity, unreasonable groups and political pressure, under participation and unprofitiablity dimensions of occupational stress.

(24) Institutional plans and policies dimensions of job-satisfaction have (*i*) positive, average and significant relation with role ambiguity, role conflict, unreasonable group and political pressure, poor peer relations, intrinsic impoverishment, low status, strenuous working condition dimensions of occupational stress; (*ii*) has positive, low but significant correlation with role overload, under participation, powerlessness dimensions of occupational stress; (*iii*) has positive, negligible but significant correlation with responsibility for persons and unprofitiability dimensions of occupational stress.

(25) Satisfaction with authorities dimension of job-satisfaction has: (*i*) positive, low but significant correlation with role overload, role ambiguity, role conflict, unreasonable group and political pressure, under participation, powerlessness, poor peer relations and intrinsic impoverishment and low status dimensions of occupational stress; (*ii*) has positive, average and significant relation with strenuous working condition dimension of occupational stress.

(26) Satisfaction with social status and welfare has: (*i*) positive, average and significant relation with intrinsic impoverishment, strenuous working conditions dimensions of occupational stress; (*ii*) has positive, negligible but significant correlation with unreasonable groups and political pressure and unprofitability dimensions of occupational stress; (*iii*) has positive, low but significant relation with role over load, role ambiguity, role conflict, under participation, powerlessness, poor peer relation and low status dimensions of occupational stress.

(27) Rapport with students dimension of job-satisfaction has: (*i*) positive, low but significant, correlation with role overload, unreasonable groups and political pressure, under participation, powerlessness and unprofitability dimensions of occupational stress; (*ii*) has positive, negligible but insignificant relation with responsibility for persons dimension of occupational stress; (*iii*) positive, average and significant relation with role ambiguity, role conflict, poor peer relation intrinsic impoverishment, low status and strenuous working condition dimensions of occupational stress.

(28) Relationship with workers dimension of job-satisfaction has: (*i*) positive, average but significant correlation with role conflict, intrinsic impoverishment and strenuous working condition dimensions of occupational stress; (*ii*) has positive, low but significant correlation with role overload, role ambiguity, unreasonable, poor peer relations and low status dimensions of occupational stress.

Discussion

Promotional avenues, service conditions and salary of primary school teachers affect their role conflict. If teachers are provided with promotional facilities, favourable service conditions and good salary, then they won't be in role conflict. Teachers will be free from external stresses and tensions and can concentrate on the problems of students and creatively, efficiently solve the problems in tribal area. If institutional plans and policies are properly framed, then teachers will not experience role ambiguity, role conflict. Institutional plan and policies are properly framed then teachers do not experience role ambiguity and role conflict, unreasonable groups and political pressure, poor peer relations, low status and strenuous working conditions of teaching profession.

If teachers remain satisfied with higher authorities (headmaster/ principals, circle inspectors, district inspector etc), and have good rapport with students, then they don't feel their working conditions is strenuous or role ambiguity or role conflict. So, good dealings of authority are very essential. Teachers should develop good rapport in tribal area so that they will come to know the problems children experience in their family, society and education. Findings of Kolte (1978), Chokker (1995) support the present study's findings.

B. Findings based on results of correlation between professional commitment and dimensions of occupational stress.

(29) Professional commitment has: (i) positive, average and significant relation with under participation dimension of job-satisfaction;(ii) has positive, low but significant co-relation with role overload, role ambiguity, role conflict, unreasonable group and political pressure, powerlessness, poor peer relations, intrinsic impoverishment, low status and strenuous working condition dimension of occupational stress;(iii) has positive, negligible but significant correlation with responsibility for persons and unprofitability dimensions of occupational stress.

Discussion

Under participation, role overload, role ambiguity, role conflict, unreasonable group and political pressure, powerlessness poor-peer relations, intrinsic impoverishment, low status and strenuous working conditions dimension of occupational stress affect teacher's commitment positively. This finding is supported by Teo, Claire and others (2002) indirectly.

C. Findings based on results of co-relation between professional commitment and dimensions of job-satisfaction.

(30) Professional commitment has: (i) positive, low but significant relation with intrinsic aspect of the job, institutional plans and politics, satisfaction with authorities satisfaction with social status and family welfare rapport with students' dimensions of job-satisfaction;(ii) has positive, negligible and significant relation with relationship with co-workers dimension of job-satisfaction.

Discussion

Intrinsic aspect of the job, institutional plans and policies, satisfaction with authorities, satisfaction with social status and family welfare and rapport with students affect teacher's commitment. These findings are directly and indirectly supported by Joshi (1999) and Yousef (2002).

D. Findings based on results of correlation among occupational stress, job-satisfaction and professional commitment.

(31) Professional commitment is positively, significantly correlated with job-satisfactions well as with occupational stress. So, professional commitment has effect on both job-satisfaction and occupational stress.

Discussion

In the present study, professional commitment is positively correlated with occupational stress and job-satisfaction of primary school teachers in tribal area. Committed teachers in tribal area want not only cent per cent enrolment, retention of tribal children in the primary education but also bring all round development of the children in these areas.

EDUCATIONAL IMPLICATIONS

The teacher is the heart and soul of education system. He should be free from all sorts of obstacles, which try to lessen his commitment to the profession, create occupational stress and make dissatisfaction in his job. In tribal areas, some factors or situations directly or indirectly affect the elementary education; so government and educational policy makers should give more attention to these factors such as physical facilities (availability of rooms, audio-visual aids, electricity facility, accommodation facility for outside teachers, residential schools in inaccessible areas of tribal districts, etc) and provide adequate staff for different classes.

High professionally committed teachers' exhibit high job-satisfaction as well as high occupational stress than low professionally committed teachers. So, it is pertinent that if teachers remain committed to their profession naturally a number of stresses come to their path but they take all those stresses positively. They try their best to improve their capabilities, qualities and efficiencies to meet the situation. Professionally committed teachers instead of horrifying and feeling strain get more job-satisfaction by overcoming obstacles. Dream of cent per cent literacy can be achieved in reality in India and tribal children can be brought to mainstream, if professionally committed teachers get appointed in primary schools.

A teacher faces peculiar situation in tribal area. But teachers who remain in tribal area for a long period become acquainted with all types of situations, so they rarely experience stress. So, frequent transfer of the teachers should be banned. Transfer provision should be made in such a way that, it should not be too short or too long. Experienced teachers face less occupational stress in tribal area. So, experienced teachers should be sent to the tribal area for primary schools to cope with the adverse situations and to handle the disinterested students properly.

Teachers should develop good rapport with students and maintain good relationship with co-workers and higher authorities. Then, they can overcome problems in their way and reduce stress of role conflict and strenuous working conditions to a large extent. No doubt to make teachers professionally committed, government should give attention to salary, promotional avenues, service conditions, physical facilities, institutional plans and policies, which directly or indirectly, create stress in teaching profession.

Parental counseling plays a vital role in tribal area for sending their children to school and to retain them. For parent teachers meetings, teachers should be accompanied by other influential members of the community to change the mindset of the tribal people towards education, so that more and more tribal people will send their children to schools and keep them in school up to the completion of their classes instead of calling their children for doing livelihood work (collection of wood from jungle, garnering Mahula, harvesting crops, taking care of their small babies etc.).

Language plays a crucial role in teaching. In tribal area, elementary education should be imparted in their regional language. No doubt, government has taken a number of initiatives regarding this, yet teachers in tribal area should be given orientation programme in tribal language. Teachers should properly accomplish this programme otherwise they should be debarred from increment and other facilities, as provided by Orissa government. With the passage of time, teachers should be refreshed academically, oriented to the new techniques and methods of teaching. This will be helpful to make the teaching effective and interesting to the tribal children.

Shiksha Sahayakas are appointed in primary schools but in tribal areas the number of Shiksha Sahayakas, those who particularly belong to tribal region, are very limited. So, in training colleges, candidates belonging to tribal area should be trained for primary schools. During training they should be motivated, given awareness about various problems of tribal people. They should come out as efficient, competent teachers to mitigate the problems in tribal area.

Circle inspectors, district inspectors of education should co-operate the teachers in every problem of the tribal area. In schools, authorities and teacher's organizations should try to have more interaction with teachers as well as should create more opportunities for communications among members of the staff by organizing informal social gatherings and various kinds of extra-curricular activities for teachers with the aim to promote mutual understanding and concern among teachers. The headmaster or circle inspectors or district inspectors should actively participate in these activities and try to establish a friendly and supportive relationship with the staff.

Government should take care to lessen the heavy workload of teachers by lifting some of the non-teaching duties like distribution of photo identity cards, BPL card and census work etc.

Orientation programmes, seminars, symposium, workshops should be organized by government as well as teacher's organizations to orient the young, inexperienced teachers with the problems of tribal area. On this occasion, teachers should get the opportunity to share their problems of how to tackle these situations.

Teachers should be rewarded for their goods deeds; this will make the teachers committed to their professions and for the sake of honour they will themselves tackle many problems in tribal area.

Primary school teachers should be provided teaching aids and resources for different subjects so that more and more tribal children are attracted towards schools.

Suggestions for Further Research

The present study has been directed towards studying occupational stress and job satisfaction in relation to professional commitment and background factors of primary schools teachers in tribal area. The study can be replicated in other ways as follow:

- Similar studies can be conducted in other States having tribal population rather than Orissa.
- A comparative study can be undertaken to see the difference in professional commitment of tribal and non-tribal school teachers at different levels of education.
- A similar study can be undertaken by taking the other variable like mobility pattern and turn-over etc.
- This study can be conduced using other methodologies, population and settings.
- There is urgent need of conducting a national level study "How to measure professional commitment of teachers" if we want to improve educational system from grassroot level.

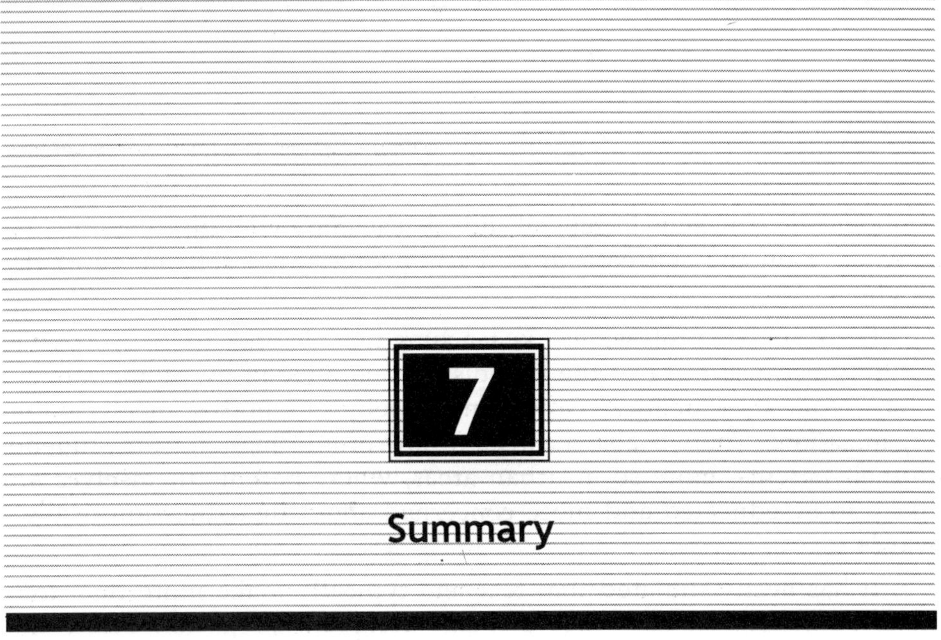

7 Summary

Statement of the Problem

"OCCUPATIONAL STRESS AND JOB SATISFACTION IN RELATION TO PROFESSIONAL COMMITMENT AND BACKGROUND FACTORS IN PRIMARY SCHOOL TEACHERS OF TRIBAL AREAS".

Justification of the Study

Education is the basic necessity like food, clothes and shelter. But our country is lagging behind to provide this basic necessity in spite of its efforts. The literacy rate in most states has not been found satisfactory even after five decades since independence. The situation is worse in tribal areas. Although the number of primary schools has increased 2.82 times since 1951 and enrolments have improved, yet the responsibility of the government by creating a satisfactory infrastructure has in practice not been matched by corresponding outlays. Primary education in India is not only suffering from inadequate allocation of resources but there is also lacking proper management and organization. Teachers are much maligned but not much attention has been given in research to the status and role, the concerns and anxieties, the satisfaction and dissatisfactions of Indian teachers in the face of growing criticism, social pressure and poor economic returns. In the face of growing public criticism, there is a need to try to understand why young enthusiastic teachers turn into bored and aloof professionals in a few years time, why many of our teachers are apathetic and uninvolved and make no effort to improve their scholarship while some others placed in the same milieu are enthusiastic, committed and show a constant desire to grow professionally. We should be concerned about the potential consequences that declining public confidence in education in general and the teaching community in particular may have on the self-esteem and the professional self-image of the teachers.

There are few professions like teaching that are open to intense public scrutiny because most of the schools are maintained by public money, funds from state or local Government, religious bodies or charitable organizations. There is also a constant flow of information from students to their parents, more so in urban areas, where parents themselves are likely to be educated and more concerned about the education of their wards.

It has been estimated that teachers typically make more than four hundred decisions a day. They dispense acceptance, rejection, praise and reproof on a whole scale basis. Many occupations or professions are distinct on this point from teaching. It is sobering to think that any one of these decisions may have either a short or long-range positive or negative influence upon a given student.

Teachers in India are increasingly facing a condescending attitude from both pupils and parents in rural, urban and tribal areas. That is why the investigator was anxious to investigate stress in teaching—what are the determinants of occupational stress, why teachers are not satisfied with their job, why teachers are not committed to their occupation. This is a matter of great concern as the teacher is the centre of the grand opera of teaching learning and the whole system revolves around him.

Primary school teachers particularly in tribal areas face a lot of stresses in teaching. In tribal areas, there are many factors like poor facilities, lack of advancement, uncongenial working conditions, handling disinterested students, local language barriers etc. Due to these stresses, teachers want to migrate from tribal areas to other areas, take leave showing false reasons and moreover, irregular attendance of the teachers is seen in many schools. That is why the present investigator wants to get answers to the following questions especially related to teachers working in tribal areas:

- Do the teachers face stress in teaching?
- Are the teachers satisfied with their occupation?
- Are the teachers committed to their profession?

If the teachers are not free from stress, and are not satisfied and committed to their profession, then the causes shall be found out. On the basis of the findings of these questions, policy makers, government and educationists will possess strong background to provide better educational system for their upliftment.

OPERATIONAL DEFINITIONS OF THE TERMS USED

Occupational Stress

Occupational stress is the stress, which employees perceive arising from various constituent and conditions of their job. Here, some factors of the job life which cause stress in some way or the other are role overload, role ambiguity, role conflict, group and political pressures, responsibility for persons, under participation, powerlessness, poor peer relations, intrinsic improvement, low status, strenuous working condition and unprofitability.

Job-satisfaction

Job-satisfaction is an attitude, which results from balancing and summation of many specific likes and dislike experiences in connection with job. In this study, the major factors of the job-satisfaction of teachers are: (*a*) intrinsic aspect; (*b*) salary, service conditions and promotion; (*c*) physical facilities; (*d*) institutional plans and policies; (*e*) satisfaction with authorities; (*f*) social status and family welfare; (*g*) rapport with students; and (*h*) relationship with co-workers.

Professional Commitment

Professional commitment means the consistency in the lines of actions undertaken regarding any profession. Consistency in teaching profession is called professional commitment of teachers. Commitment of teachers can be measured from following indicators:

(a) Positive Indicators

1.Awareness of the duties of a teacher; 2. Academic competence and will to improve upon it; 3. Awareness of the latest methods of teaching i.e. professional competence and will to improve upon it; 4. Understanding of the child psychology; 5. Interest in the whole some development of the personality of the students; 6. Patience and sympathy with the students; 7. Tactfulness and resourcefulness; 8. Punctuality and regularity; 9. Sincerity; 10. An idea of the management of time in order to cover the syllabus and do justice to each topic; 11. Able to control the class and maintain discipline; 12. Commanding respect from the students; 13. Making efforts to keep in touch with the parents for the benefit of the students; 14. Helping in administrative work; 15. Helping in organizing Co-curricular activities; 16. Job-satisfaction and feeling of pleasure in performing role as a teacher; 17. Will to continue in the teaching profession; 18. A dependable and willing worker; 19. A person with strong character.

(b) Negative Indicators

1. Refusal to take up more gainful job or occupation; 2. Sacrifice of one's own leisure time; 3. Sacrifice of money; 4. Minimization of one's own needs; 5. Neglect of one's own family; 6. Control over one's temper; 7. Sacrifice of one's own pleasure; 8. Less critical of others.

Background Factors

The following background factors will be taken into consideration:

1. Sex
2. Size of family: Number of members dependent on the teacher.
3. Teaching experience
4. Service in tribal areas
5. Socio-economic Status: In this study, educational qualification, income of the teacher's parents, spouse as well as the teacher himself are taken into consideration determining socio-economic status.

Objectives of the Study

- ➢ To develop professional commitment scale for primary school teachers.
- ➢ To know the level of job-satisfaction, occupational stress and professional commitment of primary school teachers in tribal areas.
- ➢ To study the relationship between occupational stress and professional commitment in primary school teachers in tribal areas.
- ➢ To study the relationship between job-satisfaction and professional commitment in primary school teachers in tribal areas.
- ➢ To study the relationship between job satisfaction and occupational stress in primary school teachers in tribal areas.
- ➢ To study main and interactional effects of professional commitment on occupational stress among primary school teachers in relation to following background factors:
    - Sex
    - Marital status
    - Teaching experience
    - Service in tribal area
    - Family size
    - Socio-economic status

- ➢ To study main and interaction effects of professional commitment on job-satisfaction in primary school teachers in relation to above background factors.

Hypotheses of the Study

On the basis of the objective of the study and scanning of the concerned literature, the following hypotheses were framed:

- ➢ The teachers in tribal areas have average level of occupational stress, job-satisfaction and professional commitment
- ➢ There exists positive significant relationship between occupational stress and professional commitment.
- ➢ There exists positive significant relationship between job-satisfaction and professional commitment.
- ➢ There exists significant relationship between job satisfaction and occupational stress.
- ➢ There exist significant main and interactional effects of professional commitment on occupational stress among primary school teachers in tribal area in relation to following background factors:
  - Sex
  - Marital status
  - Teaching experience
  - Service in tribal area
  - Family size
  - Socio-economic status
- ➢ There exist significant main and interactional effects of professional commitment on job satisfaction among primary school teachers in tribal area in relation to above background factors.

Delimitations of the Study

As human behaviour is a vast study, it can't be studied to global scale at a time. So, the researcher has to delimit the problem under investigation up to a certain extent, otherwise it is not possible to control all the factors involved in it. The present study has some delimitations that were presented as under:

- ➢ The study will be confined to primary school teachers teaching in tribal areas of Orissa State.
- ➢ The study will be confined to study of occupational stress, job satisfaction, professional commitment and background factors of teachers.

➢ The sample will be limited to teachers in four tribal districts i.e. Bolangir, Sambalpur, Kandhamal, Koraput of Orissa(India).

Sample

For the present study, a sample of 400 primary school teachers belonging to tribal areas of Orissa state was selected using random sampling. These 400 school teachers include both male and female teachers teaching in various types of schools from Kandhamal, Bolangir, Sambalpur, Koraput districts of Orissa(India).

Tools Used

Tools are selected for the collection of data keeping in mind the objectives of the study, variables undertaken for the study, dimensions of the variables etc. Taking into consideration all these factors, the researcher decided to use the following tools:

(*a*) Occupational Stress Index by Dr. A.K. Srivastava and Dr. A.P. Singh

(*b*) Job Satisfaction Scale by Dr. (Mrs.) Meera Dixit

(*c*) Professional Commitment Scale (Self prepared)

(*d*) Socio-economic Status Scale by S.N. Rao.

Method

Keeping in view the nature of the study, researcher has used survey method to describe and interpret what exists at present in terms of relationship and differences in occupational stress, job satisfaction and professional commitment of primary school teachers in tribal areas.

Data Collection and Scoring

The investigator visited the schools personally and administered the tools to the teachers with a request to give their responses against all the items of the tools separately. They were not only explained the purpose and significance of collecting required information from them but also made them clear that the information collected would be kept confidential and utilized for research purpose only. The teachers showed keen interest and involvement to go through each item sincerely and carefully. The investigator told the teachers to put mark (✓) against any of the five choices SD (strongly disagree), D (disagree), U (undecided), SA (strongly agree) and A (agree) for each statement as they think the most appropriate answer. The investigator convinced the unwilling teachers also about the purpose of the study and was successful in collecting data even from them.

After data collection, scoring was done on a five-point scale from one to five (1to5) for all the three scales. For the response of 'Strongly Agree' scoring is 1, for 'Agreed' it is 2, for 'Undecided' 3 marks are allotted, for 'Disagree' scoring is 4 and for 'Strongly Disagree' it is 5.The job-satisfaction score, occupational stress score and professional commitment score was the summation of scores on all the items of the scales. In job-satisfaction and occupational stress scales, scoring was done dimension-wise.

Categorisation

Profession commitment is categorized as high commitment teacher & low commitment; service in tribal areas as long service in tribal areas and short service in tribal areas; teaching experience as more teaching experience and less teaching experience; socio-economic status as high SES, middle SES, low SES; sex as male and female; marital status as married and unmarried.

Statistical Techniques Used

In the present study, mean, median, percentiles, P33, P66 and SD were used to know the nature of the data and for further analysis and interpretation skewness and kurtosis, correlation and ANOVA technique were used.

Main Findings

Main findings of the study are given in the following sections in the light of the interpretation of the results.

SECTION-A : (A) FINDINGS BASED ON NATURE OF DATA

(1) From the mean and standard deviation of scores, it is inferred that primary school teachers in tribal area have average level of job-satisfaction, moderate to high level of occupational stress and are highly committed to their profession.

SECTION-B : FINDINGS BASED ON ANALYSIS OF VARIANCE

(A) Mean differences in job satisfaction of teachers in relation to professional commitment, sex and marital status.

(2) There exists a significant difference between high and low professional commitment teachers on job-satisfaction. The mean scores indicate that high professionally committed teachers exhibit high degree of job-satisfaction as compared to low professionally committed teachers.

(3) There is significant three-factor interaction of sex, marital status and professional commitment on teacher's job-satisfaction.

(4) Other main effect such as sex and marital status and interactional effect i.e. sex and marital status, sex and professional commitment, marital and professional commitment do not exhibit significant difference on job-satisfaction of teachers.

(B) Mean differences in occupational stress of teachers in it in relation to professional commitment, sex and marital status.

(5) There is significant difference in occupational stress of high and low professional commitment teachers. The mean values show that high professionally committed teachers have high occupational stress as compared to low professionally committed teachers.

(6) There exists significant three factors interactional effect of sex, marital status and professional commitment on occupational stress of the teachers.

(7) Other main effects such as sex and marital status and interactional effects i.e. sex and professional commitment, marital status and sex, marital status and professional commitment do not exhibit significant difference on occupational stress of teachers.

(C) Mean differences in job satisfaction of teachers in relation to professional commitment, teaching experience and service in tribal area.

(8) There is significant difference in job satisfaction between teachers having long service in tribal area and short service in tribal area. The mean values indicate that those teachers who serve for a long time in tribal area have low job satisfaction than the teachers serving for a short period of time.

(9) There exists significant difference in job satisfaction of teachers belonging to high and low professional commitment. The mean scores reflect that high professionally committed teachers have more job satisfaction as compared to low professionally committed teachers.

(10) There is significant difference in job satisfaction of teaches in three-factor interaction i.e. teaching experience, service in tribal area and professional commitment.

(11) Other main effect such as teaching experience and two-factor interactional effects i.e. teaching experience and professional commitment, service in tribal area and professional commitment, teaching experience and service in tribal area do not exhibit significant difference on job-satisfaction of teachers.

(D) Mean differences in occupational stress of teachers in relation to professional commitment, teaching experience and service in tribal area.

(12) There is significant difference in occupational stress of teachers having more teaching experience and less teaching experience. The mean values show that teachers having more teaching experience exhibit less occupational stress as compared to the teachers of less teaching experience.

(13) Teachers who are serving in tribal area for long and short time show significant effect on occupational stress. The mean scores of occupational stress reveal that the teachers of long service in tribal area experience less occupational stress as compared to the teachers of short service in tribal area.

(14) There is significant two-factor interaction of teaching experience and service in tribal area on teacher's occupational stress.

(15) There exists significant three-factor interaction of teaching experience, service in tribal area and professional commitment on teachers' occupational stress.

(16) Other main effect i.e. professional commitment and interactional effects such as teaching experience and professional commitment, service in tribal area and professional commitment do not exhibit significant difference on occupational stress of teachers.

(E) Mean differences in job satisfaction of teachers in relation to professional commitment, socio-economic status and family size.

(17) There exists significant difference in job-satisfaction of high and low professional commitment teachers. The mean scores reveal that high professional committed teachers have high job satisfaction as compared to the teachers of low professional commitment.

(18) Other main effects i.e. socio-economic status, family size and two factors interactional effects such as socio-economic status and professional commitment, socio-economic status and family size, professional commitment and family size; three factor interactional effect of professional commitment, family size and socio-economic status do not exhibit significant differences on job-satisfaction of teachers.

(F) Mean Differences in Occupational Stress in Relation to Professional Commitment, Socio-economic Status and Family Size.

(19) There exists significant difference in occupational stress of high and low professional commitment teachers. The mean scores reveal that high professional committed teachers exhibit high occupational stress as compared to the teachers of low professional commitment.

(20) Other main effects i.e. socio-economic status, family size and two factors interactional effects such as socio-economic status and professional commitment, socio-economic status and family size, professional commitment and family size; three factor interactional effect of professional commitment, family size and socio-economic status do not exhibit significant differences on occupational stress of teachers.

SECTION-C : (A) FINDINGS BASED ON CORRELATION BETWEEN DIMENSIONS OF JOB-SATISFACTION AND DIMENSIONS OF OCCUPATIONAL STRESS

Main findings are as follow:

(21) Intrinsic aspect of the job satisfaction has: (*i*) average, positive but significant relation with intrinsic impoverishment and strenuous working condition dimensions of occupational stress; (*ii*) has positive, low but significant relation with role overload, role ambiguity, role conflict, under participation, powerlessness, poor peer relations, and low status dimensions of occupational stress; (*iii*) has positive, negligible but significant correlation with unreasonable groups and political pressure, unprofitability dimensions of occupational stress.

(22) Salary, promotional avenues and service conditions dimensions of job-satisfaction have: (*i*) positive, very high and significant correlation with role conflict; (*ii*) has positive, low but significant correlation with role overload, unreasonable group and political pressure, responsibility for persons, intrinsic impoverishment, low status, strenuous working condition and unprofitability dimensions of occupational stress; (*iii*) has positive, negligible but significant correlation with role ambiguity dimension of occupational stress.

(23) Physical facilities dimensions of job-satisfaction have: (*i*) positive, average and significant co-relation with intrinsic impoverishment dimension of occupational stress; (*ii*) has positive, low and significant relation with poor peer relation, low status and strenuous working conditions dimensions of occupational stress; (*iii*) has positive, negligible but significant relation with role overload, role ambiguity, unreasonable groups and political pressure, under participation and unprofitiablity dimensions of occupational stress.

(24) Institutional plans and policies dimensions of job-satisfaction have: (*i*) positive, average and significant relation with role ambiguity, role conflict, unreasonable group and political pressure, poor peer relations, intrinsic impoverishment, low status, strenuous working condition dimensions of occupational stress; (*ii*) has positive, low

but significant correlation with role overload, under participation, powerlessness dimensions of occupational stress; (*iii*) has positive, negligible but significant correlation with responsibility for persons and unprofitiability dimensions of occupational stress.

(25) Satisfaction with authorities dimension of job-satisfaction has: (*i*) positive, low but significant correlation with role overload, role ambiguity, role conflict, unreasonable group and political pressure, under participation, powerlessness, poor peer relations and intrinsic impoverishment and low status dimensions of occupational stress; (*ii*) has positive, average and significant relation with strenuous working condition dimension of occupational stress.

(26) Satisfaction with social status and welfare has: (*i*) positive, average and significant relation with intrinsic impoverishment, strenuous working conditions dimensions of occupational stress; (*ii*) has positive, negligible but significant correlation with unreasonable groups and political pressure and unfrofitability dimensions of occupational stress; (*iii*) has positive, low but significant relation with role over load, role ambiguity, role conflict, under participation, powerlessness, poor peer relation and low status dimensions of occupational stress.

(27) Rapport with students dimension of job-satisfaction has: (*i*) positive, low but significant, correlation with role overload, unreasonable groups and political pressure, under participation, powerlessness and unprofitability dimensions of occupational stress; (*ii*) has positive, negligible but insignificant relation with responsibility for persons dimension of occupational stress; (*iii*) positive, average and significant relation with role ambiguity, role conflict, poor peer relation intrinsic impoverishment, low status and strenuous working condition dimensions of occupational stress.

(28) Relationship with workers dimension of job-satisfaction has: (*i*) positive, average but significant correlation with role conflict, intrinsic impoverishment and strenuous working condition dimensions of occupational stress; (*ii*) has positive, low but significant correlation with role overload, role ambiguity, unreasonable, poor peer relations and low status dimensions of occupational stress.

(B) Findings based on results of correlation between professional commitment and dimensions of occupational stress.

(29) Professional commitment has: (*i*) positive, average and significant relation with underparticipation dimensions of job-satisfaction; (*ii*) has positive, low but significant co-relation with role overload, role ambiguity, role conflict, unreasonable group and political pressure,

powerlessness, poor peer relations, intrinsic impoverishment, low status and strenuous working condition dimensions of occupational stress; (*iii*) has positive, negligible but significant correlation with responsibility for persons and unprofitability dimensions of occupational stress.

(C) Findings based on results of correlation between professional commitment and dimensions of job satisfaction.

Professional commitment has: (*i*) positive, low but significant relation with intrinsic aspect of the job, institutional plans and politics, satisfaction with authorities satisfaction with social status and family welfare rapport with students' dimensions of job-satisfaction;(*ii*) has positive, negligible and significant relation with relationship with co-workers dimension of job-satisfaction.

(D) Findings based on results of corelation among occupational stress, job-satisfaction and professional commitment.

Professional commitment is positively and significantly correlated with job-satisfactions as well as with occupational stress. So, professiônal commitment has effect on both job-satisfaction and occupational stress of the teachers in tribal areas.

EDUCATIONAL IMPLICATIONS

The teacher is the heart and soul of education system. He should be free from all sorts of obstacles, which try to lessen his commitment to the profession, create occupational stress and make dissatisfaction in his job. In tribal areas, some factors or situations directly or indirectly affect the elementary education; so government and educational policy makers should give more attention to these factors such as physical facilities (availability of rooms, audio-visual aids, electricity facility, accommodation facility for outside teachers, residential schools in inaccessible areas of tribal districts, etc) and provide adequate staff for different classes.

High professionally committed teachers' exhibit high job-satisfaction as well as high occupational stress than low professionally committed teachers. So, it is pertinent that if teachers remain committed to their profession naturally a number of stresses come to their path but they take all those stresses positively. They try their best to improve their capabilities, qualities and efficiencies to meet the situation. Professionally committed teachers instead of horrifying and feeling strain get more job-satisfaction by overcoming obstacles. Dream of cent percent literacy can be achieved in reality in India and tribal children can be brought to mainstream, if professionally committed teachers get appointed in primary schools.

A teacher faces peculiar situation in tribal area. But teachers who remain in tribal area for a long period become acquainted with all types of situations, so they rarely experience stress. So, frequent transfer of the teachers should be banned. Transfer provision should be made in such a way that, it should not be too short or too long. Experienced teachers face less occupational stress in tribal area. So, experienced teachers should be sent to the tribal area for primary schools to cope with the adverse situations and to handle the disinterested students properly. Teachers should develop good rapport with students and maintain good relationship with co-workers and higher authorities. Then, they can overcome problems in their way and reduce stress of role conflict and strenuous working conditions to a large extent. No doubt to make teachers professionally committed, government should give attention to salary, promotional avenues, service conditions, physical facilities, institutional plans and policies, which directly or indirectly, create stress in teaching profession. Parental counseling plays a vital role in tribal area for sending their children to school and to retain them. For parent teachers meetings, teachers should be accompanied by other influential members of the community to change the mindset of the tribal people towards education, so that more and more tribal people will send their children to schools and keep them in school up to the completion of their classes instead of calling their children for doing livelihood work (collection of wood from jungle, garnering Mahula, harvesting crops, taking care of their small babies etc.).Language plays a crucial role in teaching. In tribal area, elementary education should be imparted in their regional language. No doubt, government has taken a number of initiatives regarding this, yet teachers in tribal area should be given orientation programme in tribal language. Teachers should properly accomplish this programme otherwise they should be debarred from increment and other facilities, as provided by Orissa government. With the passage of time, teachers should be refreshed academically, oriented to the new techniques and methods of teaching. This will be helpful to make the teaching effective and interesting to the tribal children.

Shiksha Sahayakas are appointed in primary schools but in tribal areas the number of Shiksha Sahayakas, those who particularly belong to tribal region, are very limited. So, in training colleges, candidates belonging to tribal area should be trained for primary schools. During training they should be motivated, given awareness about various problems of tribal people. They should come out as efficient, competent teachers to mitigate the problems in tribal area.

Circle inspectors, district inspectors of education should co-operate the teachers in every problem of the tribal area. In schools, authorities and teacher's organizations should try to have more interaction with teachers as well as should create more opportunities for communications among members of the staff by organizing informal social gatherings and various kinds of extra- curricular activities for teachers with the aim to promote mutual understanding and concern among teachers. The headmaster or circle inspectors or district inspectors should actively participate in these activities and try to establish a friendly and supportive relationship with the staff. Government should take care to lessen the heavy workload of teachers by lifting some of the non-teaching duties like distribution of photo identity cards, BPL card and census work etc.

Orientation programmes, seminars, symposium, workshops should be organized by government as well as teacher's organizations to orient the young, inexperienced teachers with the problems of tribal area. On this occasion, teachers should get the opportunity to share their problems of how to tackle these situations. Teachers should be rewarded for their goods deeds; this will make the teachers committed to their professions and for the sake of honour they will themselves tackle many problems in tribal area. Primary school teachers should be provided teaching aids and resources for different subjects so that more and more tribal children are attracted towards schools.

Suggestions for Further Research

The present study has been directed towards studying occupational stress and job satisfaction in relation to professional commitment and background factors of primary schools teachers in tribal area. The study can be replicated in other ways as follow:

- Similar studies can be conducted in other States having tribal population rather than Orissa.
- A comparative study can be undertaken to see the difference in professional commitment of tribal and non-tribal school teachers at different levels of education.
- A similar study can be undertaken by taking the other variable like mobility pattern and turn-over etc.
- This study can be conduced using other methodologies, population and settings.
- There is urgent need of conducting a National level study "How to measure professional commitment of teachers" if we want to improve educational system from grass root level.

Bibliography

Abraham, A. (1986). Study of Organizational Climate of Government High School of Chandigarh and Its Effect on Job Satisfaction of Teacher, *Ph.D. Thesis*, Punjab University.

Abu Saad, I. & Isralowitz, R. E. (1992). Teachers' Job Satisfaction in Transitional Society within the Bedouin Arab Schools of the Negev. *The Journal of Social Psychology,* 132 (6), 771-781.

Adeyemo, D.A. (1997). Relative Influence of Gender and Working Experience on Job Satisfaction of Primary School Teachers. *The Primary School Educators, 1, 1,* 86-89.

Adeyemo, D.A. (2000). Job Involvement, Career Commitment, Organizational Commitment and Job Satisfaction of the Nigerian Police. A Multiple Regression Analysis. *Journal of Advance Studies in Educational Management 5(6),* 35-41.

Adeyemo, D.A. & Aremu, A.O. (1999). Career Commitment Among Secondary School Teachers in Oyo State, Nigeria. The Role of biographical mediators. *Nigerian Journal of Applied Psychology 5 (2),* 184-194.

Adval, S. B.;Kekkar, A; Agarwal, M.J. & Gupta, S.B. (1961). Causes of Failure in High School Examination. *Department of Education,* Allahbad University.

Ahmed, Q. (1986). Determinants of Job Involvement Among Teachers. *Ph.D. Thesis,* Magadh University.

Ajalal,P. & Raju, S.(2004).Employee Morale and Achievement Motivation of Public and Private Sector Employees in Kerala. Journal of Community Guidance and Research, 21 (2),.206-212.

Akkinnusi, D.M. (1994) Relationship Between Personal Attributes, Stressors, Stress Reactions and Coping Styles. Management and Labour Studies, 19(4), 211-218.

Aluja, A., Blanch, A. & Garcia, L.F. (2005). Dimensionality of the Maslach Burnout Inventory in School Teachers: A Study of Several Proposals. *European Journal of Psychological Assessment,* 21 (1), 67-76.

Angle, H., & Perry, J. (1981). An Empirical Assessment of Organizational Commitment and Organizational Effectiveness. *Administrative Science Quarterly,* 26, 1-14.

Annamalai, A.R. (1999). A Study of Job Satisfaction of Teachers in Relation to Certain Selected Variables. Indian Educational Abstract, 5 (8), 47.

Alice M. (2005), The Occupational Stress of Teachers'. Journal of Community Guidance and Reseach, 19(4),211-218

Antony, S. (2002). Exploring the Satisfaction of Part Time College Faculty in the United States. Review of Higher Education", *Journal of the Association for the Study of Higher Education*, 26(1), 41-56.

Aranya, N., Pollock, J. & Amernic, J. (1981). An Examination of Professional Commitment in Accouting. *Accounting Organisations and Society*, 6, 271-280.

Archana, V. & Mishra,P.C.(2005).Occupational Stress and Social Support as Predictors of Affective Commitment. *Journal of Community Guidance and Research*, 22(.1), 76-80.

Armes, D. (1985). *The Unhappiest Profession*. Report for the Teachers' Joint Committee (AMMA, NAS/UMT, NUT) (available from the author, 5 Ambleside Avenue, Bradford BD9 5HX, England).

Arora, K. (1976). Difference Between Effective and Ineffective Teachers. *Ph.D Thesis*, Jamia Millia Islamia University, New Delhi.

Arthur, James (2003). Professional Value Commitments, *British Journal of Educational Studies*, ISSN 0007-1005.

Ashton, P.T., & Webb, R.B. (1986). *Making a Difference: Teachers Sense of Efficacy and Student Achievement (Research on Teaching Monograph Series)*. New York: Longman.

Australian Teaching Council. (1995). *What Do Teachers Think?* Leichhardt: Australian Teaching Council Becker, T.E, Randal, D.M, & Riegel, C.D. (1995).The Multidimensional View of Commitment and Theory of Reasoned Action: *A Comparative Evaluation: Journal of Management* 21 (4), 617–638.

Auskar, P. (1996). A Study of Job Satisfaction Among Teachers Working in Government and Private Secondary School. *The Progress of Education*, LXXI (3), 50-53.

Balwinder K. (1986). Job Satisfaction of Home Science Teachers. Its Relationship with Personal, Professional and Organizational Characteristics. *Ph.D. Thesis* .University of Punjab

Barnes, B. L. (1992b). Stress in Aviation Personnel. *Psychological Studies*, 37(1), 1-6.

Bass, B.M. (1985). *Leadership and Performance Beyond Expectations*. Free Press, New York.

Bateman, T. & Strasser, S. (1984).A Longitudinal Analysis of the Antecedents of Organizational Commitment, *Academy of Management Journal*, 27, 95-112.

Batlivala, S. (1990). Counteracting Stress. In D.M.Pestonjee (Ed.), *Stress and Coping: The Indian Experience* (2nd Ed., pp.251-287). New Delhi: Sage Publications.

Ben-Ari, R., Krole, R. & Har-Even, D. (2003). Differential Effects of Simple Frontal *vs.* Complex Teaching Strategy on Teachers' Stress, Burnout, and Satisfaction. *International Journal of Stress Management, 10 (2)*, 173-195

Bernard, M.E. (1990). *Taking the Stress Out of Teaching*. Burwood: Collins Dove.

Bhattacharji, A. (1989). Academic Stress and Attitudes of Elementary School Children Towards Homework. An Unpublished Master Thesis by J.Krishna, S.V.University, Tirupati, 1994.

Bhargava, S., & Kelkar, A. (2000). Prediction of Job Involvement, Job Satisfaction and Empowerment from Organizational Structure and Corporate Culture. *Psychological Studies*, 45 (1&2), 43-50.

Beauvois J. L., Bungert M. & Mariette P. (1995). Forced Compliance: Commitment to Compliance and Commitment to Activity, *European Journal of Social Psychology*, 25, 17-26.

Becker, H.S. (1960). Notes on Personal Commitment. *American Journal of Sociology*, 66, 32-42.

Beegam, L. & Dharmangadan, N. (2000).Gender Differences in Job Satisfaction, *Indian Psychological Abstract and Review*,10(2), 277.

Best, J.W. & Kahn (1992). *Research in Education*, New Delhi: Prentice Hall of India Pvt. Ltd.

Bhatt, D.J. (1997). Job Stress, Job Involvement and Job Satisfaction of Teachers: A Correlation Study. *Indian Educational Abstract*, July, 1, 24.

Bhatt, D.J. (2001). Job Stress, Job Involvement and Job Satisfaction of Teachers: A Correlation Study. *Indian Educational Abstract*, 1(1), 84-85, NCERT, New Delhi.

Biklen, S. K. (1995). School Work—Gender and the Cultural Construction of Teaching. New York: Teachers College Press.

Bisaria, S. (1991).*Mobility Patterns and Professional Commitments of Higher Secondary Teachers. A Pilot Study: Independent Study*, NCERT: New Delhi

Biswas, U.N. (1998).The Effect of Life Styles Stressors on Organisational Commitment. *Indian Educational Abstract*, 1(5), 57.

Biswas, U.N. (1998). Life Style Stresses, Organizational Commitment, Job Involvement and Perceived Organizational Effectiveness Across Job Levels. *Indian Journal of Industrial Relations*, 34 (1), 55-72.

Blasé, J.J. (1982). A Social-psychological Grounded Theory of Teacher Stress and Burnout. *Educational Administration Quarterly*, 18, pp. 93-113.

Blasé, J.J. (1986). A Quantitative Analysis of Sources of Teacher Stress: Consequences for Performance. *American Educational Research Journal* 23, 13-40.

Blood, G. W. & Ridenour, J. W. (2003). Predicting Job-satisfaction Among Public School, *Language, Speech and Hearing Services in Schools*, 33(47), 282-290.

Borg M.G., Riding, R.J. & Falzon, J.M.(1991). Stress in Teaching:A Study of Occupational Stress and its Determinants, Job-satisfaction and Career Commitment Among Primary School, *Teacher's Educational Psychology*. 11, 59-74.

Borg, M.G. & Riding, R.J. (1992).Occupational Stress and Satisfaction in Teaching. *British Educational Research Journal*, 17, 263-81.

Bong, M. G. & J. Riding, R. (1993).Occupational Stress and Job Satisfaction Among School Administrators, *Journal of Educational Administration*, Vol. 31, No. 1 pp. 4-21.

Borg, W.R. & Gall, M.D. (1989).*Educational Research—An Introduction*, 5th ed., Longman, Harlow.

Borg, M.G. & Falzon, J.M. (1991). Sources of Teacher Stress in Maltese Primary Schools. *Research in Education*, 46, 1-15.

Borg, M.G. & Riding, R. J. (1993). Occupational Stress and Job Satisfaction Among School Administrators. *Journal of Educational Administration*, 31 (1), 4-21.

Borg, M.G., Riding, R.J. (1991).Occupational Stress and Satisfaction in Teaching, *British Educational Research Journal*, Vol. 17, pp. 263-81.

Borg, M.G., Riding, R.J. & Falzon, J.M. (1991). Stress in Teaching: A Study of Occupational Stress and its Determinants, Job Satisfaction and Career Commitment Among Primary Schoolteachers. *Educational Psychology,* 11 (1), 59-75.

Brown, M. & Ralph, S. (1992). Towards the Identification of Stress in Teachers. *Research in Education, 48,* 103-110.

Brookover, W.B., Beady, C.H., Flood, P.K., Schweitzer, J.M., & Wisenbaker, J.M. (1979). *School Social Systems and Student Achievement,* New York: Praeger.

Brophy, J.E., & Good, T.L. (1974). *Teacher-student Relationships: Causes and Consequences.* New York: Holt, Rinehart & Winston.

Bruce, K. & Cacioppe, R. (1989). A Survey of Why Teachers Resigned from Government Secondary Schools in Western Australia. *Australian Journal of Education, 33 (1)* ,68-82.

Buch, M.B. (1974). *A Survey of Research in Education,* CASE, Baroda; MSU.

Buch, M.B. (1979) *Second Survey of Research in Education,* (1972-79), CASE, Baroda: MSU.

Buch, M.B. (1984). *Third Survey of Research in Education* (1983-1988), Vol. I &II, NCERT: New Delhi.

Buch, M.B. (1991).*Fourth Survey of Research in Education,* (1978-83), NCERT: New Delhi

Buch, M.B. (1999 & 2000). Fifth Survey of Research in Education (1988-92), Vol. I & II, NCERT: New Delhi.

Burke, R.J. & Greenglass, E. (1994). A Longitudinal Study of Psychological Burnout in Teachers. *Human Relations, 47 (3),* 1-15.

Butt, G., Lance, A., Fielding, A., Gunter, H., Rayner, S. & Thomas, H. (2005).Teacher Job Satisfaction: Lessons from the TSW Pathfinder Project. *School Leadership and Management,* 25(5), 455—71.

Caputo, J.S. (1991). *Stress and Burnout in Library Service.* Phoenix: Oryx Press.

Cambell, J. P., & Pitchard, R. D. (1977). Motivation Theory in Industrial and Organizational Psychology. In M.D.Dunnette(Ed.), *Handbook of Industrial and Organizational Psychology.* Chicago: Rand McNally.

Cammann, C. et al. (1983). Assessing the Attitudes and Perceptions of Organizational Members in Seashore, S.E.et al. (Eds), *Assessing Organisation Change,* John Weily, New York, NY, pp.71-138.

Chaplain, R.P. (1995). Stress and Job Satisfaction: A Study of English Primary School Teachers. *Educational Psychology, 15 (4),* 473-489.

Chand, P., & Sethi, A.S. (1997). Organisational Factors in the Development of Work Stress. *Indian Journal of Industrial Relations,* 32 (4), 453-462.

Chandraiah, K. (1994). Effect of Age on Job Satisfaction Among College Teachers. The Creative Psychologist, 6 (1&2), 53-56.

Cherniss, C. (1995). *Beyond Burnout: Helping Teachers, Nurses, Therapists and Lawyers Recover from Stress and Disillusionment,* Routledge, New York, NY.

Cheng, Y. C. (1990). An Investigation of Antecedents of Organisational Commitment. *Educational Research Journal,* 5, 29-42.

Cheng,Y.C. and Tsui, K.T. (1996). Total Teacher Effectiveness: New Conception and Improvement, *International Journal of Education Management,* Vol.10 No.6, pp.7-17.

Chhokar, S. (1995).The Role and Organisational Correlates of Job Satisfaction, Job Involvement, Organizational Commitment and Psychological Strain Among Bank Employees, *Indian Educational Abstract*, 1, 5-8.

Chhokar, J.S. (1995). Organisational Values, Role Demands and Job-related effective experiences in India. *Indian Journal of Industrial Relation*, 30 (4), 427-438.

Choudhary, R. (2001).*Teacher's Burnout in Relation to Occupational Stress, Mental Health Problems and Socio-economic Status a Factor Analytical Study*, Ph.D., Kurukshetra University.

Chattopadhya, I., & Dasgupta, S.K. (1999). Good News About Role Stress. *Journal of the Indian Academy of Applied Psychology*, 25 (1-2), 35-38.

Chaudhary, A. (1990). Role Stress in Special Group. In D.M.Pestonjee (Ed.), *Stress and Coping: The Indian Experience* (2nd ed., pp. 137-215). New Delhi: Sage Publication.

Cockburn, A.D. & Haydn T. (2004). Recruiting and Retaining Teachers: Understanding Why Teachers Teach. London: Routledge Falmer

Cole, R.E. (1979). *Work, Mobility and Participation.* University of California Press, Berkeley, CA.

Conger, J.A., Kanungo, R.N. and Associates (1988). *Charismatic Leadership: Elusive Factor in Organisational effectiveness*, Jossey- Bass, San Francisco, CA.

Corrigan, P.W., Holmes, E.P. & Luchins, D. (1995). Burnout and Collegial Support in State Psychiatric Hospital Staff. *Journal of Clinical Psychology, 51 (5)*, 703-710.

Cote, S. & Morgan, G. (2002). A Longitudinal Analysis of the Association Between Emotion Regulation, Job Satisfaction and Intentions to Quit. *Journal of Organisational Behaviour*, 23(8), 947-962.

Cox, T. & Brockley, T. (1984). The Experience and Effects of Stress in Teachers. *British Educational Research Journal* 10, 83-7.

Crossman, A. & Harris, P. (2006). Job Satisfaction of Secondary School Teachers. *Educational Management Administration and Leadership*, 34(1), 29—46.

Crosswell, L. (2003). The Dimensions of Teacher Commitment: the Different Ways in Which Teachers Conceptualise and Practice Their Commitment. In Singh, P. and McWilliam, E. (Eds.), Performing Research. Flaxton: Post Pressed. (in press).

Cunningham, W.G. (1983). Teacher Burnout-solutions for the 1980s: A Review of the Literature. *Urban Review* 15, 37-51.

Currivan, D.B. (2000). The Causal Order of Job Satisfaction and Organizational Commitment in Models of Employee Turnover. *Human Resource Management Review*, 9 (4), 495-524.

Daga, N. (1997). Role Stress in Special Groups. In D. M. Pestonjee (Ed.), *Stress and Coping: The Indian Experience* (2nd ed., pp. 137-215). New Delhi: Sage publication.

Daley, M.R. (1979).Burnout Smouldering Problem in Protective Services, *Social Work*, 24(5), pp.375-379.

Das, L. & Panda, B.B. (1995). Job Satisfaction of College and Higher Secondary Teachers. Experiments in Education, XXII(3), 52-56.

Davis, J. & Wilson, S.M. (2000). Principals' Efforts to Empower Teachers: Effects on Teacher Motivation and Job Satisfaction and Stress. *The Clearing House*, 73 (6), 349-353.

Day, C. (2000). Stories of Change and Professional Development: The Costs of Commitment. In C. Day & A. Fernandez & T. Hauge & J. Moller (Eds.), The Life and Work of Teachers: International Perspectives in Changing Times (pp. 109-129). London: Falmer Press.

Day, C. (2004). A Passion for Teaching. London: Routledge Falmer

Day, D.V., Bedeian, A.G. & Conte, J.M. (1998). Personality as Predictor of Work-related Outcomes: Test of a Mediated Latent Structural Model. *Journal of Applied Social Psychology*, 28, (22), 2068-2088.

De Nobile, J. (2003). *Organisational Communication, Job Satisfaction and Occupational Stress in Catholic Primary Schools.* Unpublished Doctoral Thesis, University of New South Wales, Sydney

Deosthalee, P. G. (2002).Are Indian Expatriates in Sultanate of Oman Under Stress. *Journal of Managerial Psychology*, 17(6), 523-528.

Derlin, R. & Schneider, G.T. (1994). Understanding Job Satisfaction: Principals and Teachers. Urban and Suburban. *Urban Education, 29 (1)*, 63-88.

Devraj, S. (2001) Quoted in Srikanth Reddy,V,Bala Koteswari,V and Tirumala Rao,T.(2005).Source of Stress Among Adolescents.*Journal of Community Guidance and Research*, 22(2),25-28

Dewe, P.J. (1986). An Investigation into the Causes and Consequences of Teacher Stress. *New Zealand Journal of Educational Studies* 21, 145-57.

Dinham, S. (1997). Teaching and Teacher's Families. Australian Educational Researcher

Dinham, S. (1993). Teachers Under Stress. *Australian Educational Researcher,* 20 (3), 1-16.

Dinham, S. (2004). The Changing Face of Teaching. *Professional Eductor,* 3 (2), 2-3.

Dinham, S. & Scott, C. (1998). A Three Domain Model of Teacher and School Executive Career Satisfaction.

Journal of Educational Administration, 36 (4), 362-378.

Dinham, S. & Scott, C. (2000). Moving Into the Third, Outer Domain of Teacher Satisfaction. *Journal of Educational Administration*, 38 (4), 379-396.

Dixit, M.A. (1986). *A Comparative Study of Job Satisfaction Among Primary and Secondary School Teachers.* Ph.D.(Edu)., Lucknow University.

Dixit, M. (1993). Job Satisfaction for Primary and Secondary Teachers. National Psychological Corporation.

Docking, R.A. & Docking, E. (1984).Reducing Teacher Stress. *Unicorn*, 10 (3), 261-274.

Dohrenwend, B.S. & Dohrenwend, B.P. (Eds.) (1974). *Stressful Life Event: Their Nature and Effect*, New York: Wiley.

Dornstein, M., & Matalon, Y. (1998). A Comparative Analysis of Predictors of Organizational Commitment. A Study of Voluntary Army Personnel in Isreal. *Journal of Vocational Behaviour* 34(2), 192-203.

Dubin, R. Chanpoux, J.E. & Porter, L.W. (1975).Central Life Interests and Organizational Commitment of Blue Collar and Clerical Workers. *Administrative Science Quarterly*, 20, 411-21.

Duke, D.L., Showers, B.K., & Imber, M. (1981). Studying Shared Decision Making in Schools. In S.B.Bachrach (Ed.), *Organisational Behavior in Schools and School Districts.* New York: Praeger.

Dunham,J.(1984).*Stress in Teaching*. New York, Nicholas

Dunham,J.(1986). A Decade of Stress in Teaching Research in the United Kingdom (1976-86). *School Organisation and Management Abstracts* 5, 161-73.

Dunham, J. (1998). Stress Situations and Response. In National Association of School masters (Ed.), Stress in Schools. Hemel Hempstead. (England): National Association of School Master.

Dwyer. B. (2005). *Creating Tomorrow's Catholic School: A Challenge to the Imagination*.Ann D. Clark Lecture. Catholic Education Office, Parramatta, 1st September, 2005.

Edmonds, R. (1979). Effective Schools for the Urban Poor. *Educational Leadership*, 37, 15-24.

Education and Manpower Branch and Education Department (1998). Quality Education Fund.

Elliott, B., & Crosswell, L. (2001). Commitment to Teaching: Australian Perspectives on the Interplays of the Professional and the Personal in Teachers' Lives. Paper Presented at the International Symposium on Teacher Commitment at the European Conference on Educational Research, Lille, France.

Eliophotou-Menon, M. & Saitis, C. (2006). Satisfaction of Pre-service and In-service Teachers with Primary School Organisation. Educational Management Administration and Leadership, 34(3), 345-63

Etzion, D. (1984). Moderating Effect of Social Support on the Stress-burnout Relationship. *Journal of Applied Psychology*, 69, 615-662.

Etzion, A. (1961). *A Comparative Analysis of Complex Organizations*. New York: Free Press.

Evans, L. (1998). Teacher Morale, Job Satisfaction and Motivation. London: Paul Chapman

Evans, M.G. (1986). Organisational Behaviour: The Central Role of Motivation. *Journal of Management*. 12 (2), 203.

Fair brother, K. & Warn J. (2003).Work Place Dimensions, Stress and Job Satisfaction. *Journal of Managerial Psychology*, 18(1), 8-21.

Farber, B.A. (1980). Stress and Burnout Implications for Teacher Motivation, Paper Presented at the Annual Meeting of the Area, New York: Mark.

Farber, B.A. (1984). Stress and Burnout in Sub-urban Teachers. *Journal of Educational Research*, 77, 325-331.

Farber, B.A. (1991). *Crisis in Education: Stress and Burnout in the American Teacher*. San Francisco: Jossey Bass.

Fay R. J. (2000). Job-satisfaction of Jamican Elementary School Teachers, *Psychological Abstract*, 8, 69.

Fimian, M.J. (1984). The Development of an Instrument to Measure Occupational Stress in Teachers: The Teacher Stress Inventory. *Journal of Occupational Psychology*, 57, 277-93.

Fink, S.L. (1992). *High Commitment Workplace*, Quorum Books, New York, NY.

Firestone, W. A. (1996). Images of Teaching and Proposals for Reform: A Comparison of Ideas from Cognitive and Organisational Research. *Educational Administration Quarterly*, 32(2), pp.209-235.

Firestone, W.A. & Rosenblum, S. (1988). The Alienation and Commitment of Students and Teachers in Urban Schools. Paper Presented at the Annual Meeting of the American Educational Research Association, New Orleans

Fisher, S. (1994). *Stress in Academic Life*, Press Celfic Court, Buckingham.

Fletcher, B.C. & Payne, R.L. (1982).Levels of Reported Stressors and Strains Amongst Schoolteachers, Some U.K. Data, *Educational Review*, 34, pp.267-278.

Fraser, H., Draper, J., & Taylor, W. (1998). The Quality of Teachers' Professional Lives: Teachers and Job-satisfaction. *Evaluation and Research in Education*, 12(2), pp.61-71.

Freeman, A. (1987). Pastoral Care and Teacher Stress. *Pastoral Care in Education* 5, 22-8.

Fried, R. L. (1995). The Passionate Teacher: A Practical Guide. Boston, Mass.: Beacon Press.

Friedman, I.A. & Farber, B.A. (1992). Professional self-concept as a Predictor of Teacher Burnout. *Journal of Educational Research*, 86, 28-35.

Fukami, C. & Larson, E. (1984). Commitment to company and Union; Parallel Models, *Journal of Applied Psychology*, 69, 367-371.

Galloway, D., Panckhurst, F., Buswell, K., Boswelly, C. & Green, K. (1987). Sources of Stress for Class Teachers in Newzeland Primary Schools, *Pastrola Care in Education*, 5(1), 28-36.

Galloway, D., Ball, T., Blomfield, D. & Seyd, R. (1982). *Schools and Disruptive Pupils*. Longman: London.

Garrett, R.M. (1999). Teacher Job Satisfaction in Developing Countries. Educational Research Supplemental Series (G), No. ED 459 150, ERIC Document Reproduction Service.

Gayanani, T.C. (1998). *Stress and Strain Among the Teachers Working in Higher Education Institutes of Different Organizational Climate*. Ph.D(Edu.), Agra University.

Gellis, Z. (2002).Coping with Occupational Stress in Healthcare: A Coping with Occupational Workers and Nurses: Comparison of Social Workers and Nurses, *Administration on Social Work*, 26 (3), 37-52.

Gmelth, W.H. Lovrich, N.P. and Wilke, P.K. (1984) "Sources of Stress in Academic: A National Perspective", *Research in Higher Education*, 20, 477-490.

Golaszewski, T. J., Milstein, M.M., Duquetta R.D. & London, W. M. (1984).Organisational and Health Manifestations of Teachers Stress. A preliminary Report of the Buffalo Teachers Stress Intervention Project. *Journal of School Health*, 54, 458-463.

Goldenberg, D. & Waddell, J. (1990).Occupational Stress and Coping Strategies Among Female Baccalaureate Nursing Faculty, *Journal of Advanced Nursing*, 15, 531-543.

Good, C.V. (1959). *Dictionary of Education*, New York, McGraw Hill.

Good, T.L. (1981). Teacher Expectations and Student Perceptions: A Decade of Research. *Educational Leadership*, 35, 415-422.

Good, T.L., & Brophy, J.E. (1984). *Looking in Classrooms*. New York: Harper & Row.

Goodman, P.S.., Atkin, R.S. and Associates (1984). *Absenteeism*, Jossey-Bass, San Francisco, CA.

Goyal, J.C. (1980). A Study of the Relationship Among Attitudes, Job Satisfaction, Adjustment and Professional Interests of Teacher Educators in India. Ph.D. Thesis, Delhi University.

Graham, K. C. (1996). Running Ahead: Enhancing Teacher Commitment. *Journal of Physical Education, Recreation and Dance*, 67(1), pp.45-47

Green, R. L. (1987). *Expectations: Research Implications on a Major Dimension of Effective Schooling*. Cleveland, OH: Joint Center for Applied Research and Urban education.

Griffen, R.W., & Bateman, T.S. (1986). Job Satisfaction and Organizational Commitment. In C.L.Cooper & I. Robertswon (Eds.), *International Review of Industrial and Organizational Psychology*. New York: Wiley.

Griva, K. & Joekes, K. (2003). UK Teachers under Stress: Can We Predict Wellness on the Basis of Characteristics of the Teaching Job? *Psychology and Health*, 18 (4), 457-471

Guilford, J. P. (1950).*Fundamental Statistics in Psychology and Education* New York: McGraw- Hill.

Gupta, B.L. & Pande, H.S. (1999). Commitment Level of Polytechnic Teachers and Strategies to Enhance It—A Study, I*ndian Educational Abstract*, 12(14), 47.

Gupta, N. & Beehr T.(1979).Job Stress and Employee Behaviour. *Organisational Behaviour and Human Performance*, 23, 373-387.

Harper, F. G. (1997). Job Satisfaction and Organizational Factors: A Model of Teacher Job Satisfaction for Differential Context and Career Stages. *Dissertation Abstract International*, 57 (12).

Hart, N.I. (1987). Student Teachers' Anxieties: Four Measured Factors and Their Relationships to Pupil Disruption in Class. *Educational Research* 29, 12-18.

Hanna, S. (1999).Effect of School Change Project on Teacher's Satisfaction with Their Work and Their Perceptions of Teaching Difficulties.

Hansen, J. & Sullivan, B.A. (2003). Assessment of Workplace Stress: Occupational Stress, Its Cons and Common Causes of Teacher Stress. In (unknown Ed.) *Measuring Up:Assessment Isues for Teachers, Counselors and Administrators.* ERIC Document No. ED480078.

Herzberg, F. (1968). One More Time: How Do You Motivate Employees? *Harvard Business Review*, 46, 53-62

Hiebert, B. & Farber, I. (1984). Teacher Stress: A Literature Survey with a View to Surprises. *Canadian Journal of Education* 9, 14-27.

Hrebinaik, L. G. (1974). Effects of Job Level and Participation on Employee Attitudes and Perceptions of Influence. *Academy of Management Journal*, 17, 649-662.

Hrebinaik, L. G., & Aluto, J. (1972). Personal and Role-related Factors in the Development of Organizational Commitment. *Administrative Science Quarterly*, 17, 555-572

Hodge, G.M., Jupp, J.T & Taylor, A.J. (1994). Work Stress, Distress and Burn-out in Music and Mathematics Teachers,*British Journal of Educational Psychology*, 64, 65-76.

Hogan, T. (2002), Stressors and Stress Reactions Among University Personnel, *Psychological Abstract*, 6, 127.

Holt, P., Fine, M.T. & Tellefson, N. (1987). Mediating Stress: Survival of the Bandy, *Psychology in the Schools*, 24, 51-58.

Hoy, W.K., & Ferguson, J. (1985). A Theoretical Framework and Exploration of Organizational Effectiveness of Schools. *Educational Administration Quarterly*, 21, 117-134.

Huber, M. (1999). Co-ordination within Schools, Commitment of Teachers and Students and Student Acheivement. *Educational Research and Evaluation*, 5(2), pp. 139-156.

Huberman, M. (1993). The Lives of Teachers (J. Neufeld, Trans.). London: Cassell Villiers House.

Hung, A. & Liu, J. (1999).Effects of Stayback on Teachers' Professional Commitment, *The International Journal of Educational Management*,13(15), 226-240.

Hutni, M., & Lindeman, M. (2002). The Role of Stress and Negative Emotions in an Occupational Crisis, *Journal of Career Development*, 29(1), 19-36.

Indirsean, J. (1973). Multivariate Analysis of Factors Affecting Job Satisfaction of Engineering Teacher. *Ph.D Thesis, Jamia Millia Islamia University*.

Irving , P.G., Coleman, D.F., & Cooper, C.L. (1997). Further Assessment of a Three Component Model of Occupational Commitment: Generalizability and Differences Across Occupations. *Journal of Applied Psychology* 82, 444-452.

Jamal, M. (1997). Job Stress, Satisfaction and Mental Health: An Empirical Examination of Self-employed and Non-self Employed Canadians. *Journal of Small Business Management*, 35 (4), 48-57.

James, W. K. (1992). The Organizational Dynamics of Teacher Workplace Commitment: A Study of Urban Elementary and Middle Schools. *Educational Administration Quarterly*, 28(1).

Jernigam, I.E. (2002). Dimensions of Work Satisfaction as Predictors of Commitment Type, *Journal of Managerial Psychology*, 17(7), 564-579.

Joshi, S. (1999). The Inter-relationship Between Job-satisfaction, Job Involvement and Work Involvement and Their Relationship with Age Job Experience, Monthly Income and Educational Level, Indian Educational Abstract, 2 (1-2), 73.

Kalliath, T.J. & Beck, A. (2001). Is the Path to Burn-out and Turnover Paved by a Lack of Supervisory Support? *New Zealand Journal of Psychology*, 30 (2), 72-78.

Kanter, R. M. (1974). Commitment and Social Organisation. In D. Field (Ed.), Social Psychology for sociologists (pp. 126-146). London: Nelson.

Kelchtermans, G. (1999).Teaching Career: Between Burnout and Fading Away? Reflections from a Narrative and Biographical perspective, in Vandenberghe, R., Huberman, H. (Eds),*Understanding and Preventing Teacher Burn-out: A Sourcebook of International Research and Practice*, Cambridge University Press, Cambridge, pp.176-91.

Katz, D., & Kahn, R.L. (1978). *The Social Psychology of Organizations*. New York: Wiley

Kaur B. (1986). *Job-Satisfaction of Home Science Teachers: Its Relationship with Persons Professional and Organsation Characteristic*, Ph.D (Edu.), Punjab University.

Kaur, R. (2002). *A Study of Occupational Stress Among Elementary School Teachers in Relation to Role Conflict, Job Satisfaction and Biographical Variables*, Ph.D(Edu), Kurukshetra University, Haryana.

Keinan, G. & Perlberg, A. (1907). Stress in Academic: A Cross Cultural Comparison Between Extract and American Academicians, *Journal of Cross Cultural Psychology*, 18, 193-207.

Khatoon, T. & Hasan, Z. (2000). Job-satisfaction of Secondary School Teachers in Relation to Their Personal Variables, Sex, Experience, Professional Training, Salary and Religion. *Indian Educational Abstract*, 2(1-2).

Kirkcaldy, B.D., Trimpop, Q.M. & Williams, T. (2002).Occupational Stress and Health Outcome Among British and German Managers, *Journal of Managerial Psychology,* 17(b), 491-505.

Kirkcaldy, Bruce (2002). Job Stress and Dissatisfaction Comparing Male and Female Medical Practitioners and Auxiliary Personnel, *European Review of Applied Psychology,* 52(1), 51-61.

Knutton, S. & Mycroft, A. (1986). Stress and the Deputy Head. *School Organisation* 6, 49-59.

Kobasa, S.C. (1982).Commitment and Coping in Stress Resistance Among Lawyer, *Journal of Personal Social Psychology,* 42(9), 707-717.

Koch, J., & Steers, R. (1978). Job Attachment, Satisfaction and Turnover Among Public Employees. *Journal of Vocational Behavior,* 12, 119-128.

Kotte, N.V. (1978). Job Satisfaction of Primary School Teachers. A Test of the Two Factor Theory. *National Institute of Rural Development,* Hyderabad.

Koustelios, A.D. (2001).Personal Characteristics and Job Satisfaction of Greek Teachers'. *International Journal of Educational Management* , 15(7), 354-8

Krishman, J.W. (1992). The Organisational Dynamics of Teachers Workplace Commitment: A Study of Urban Elementary and Middle Schools", *Educational Administration Quarterly,* 28(1), 5-42.

Kyriacou, C. (1989). The Nature and Prevalence of Teacher Stress. In Cole, M. and Walker, S. (Ed.s) *Teaching and Stress.* (pp. 26-34). Milton Keynes: Open UniversityPress.

Kyriacou, C. (2001). Teacher Stress: Directions for Future Research. *Educational Review,* 53 (1), 27-35.

Kyriacou, C. and Suttcliffe, J. (1977). Teacher Stress: A Review. *Educational Review,* 24 (4), 299-306.

Kyriacou, C. & Sutchiffa, J. (1979). Teacher Stress and Satisfaction, *Educational Research,* 21, 89-96.

Kyriacou, C. (1980). Coping Actions and Occupational Stress Among School Teachers, *Research in Education,* 24, 51-61.

Kyriacou, C. & Sutcliffe, J. (1977).Teacher, Stress: A Review, *Educational Review,* 29(4), 299-306.

Kyriacou, C. & Sutcliffe, J. (1978a). A Model of Teacher Stress, *Educational Study,*4(1),1-6.

Kyriacou, C. & Sutcliffe, J. (1978b).Teacher Stress: Prevalence, Sources and Symptoms, *British Journal of Educational Psychology,* 48,159-167.

Kyriancou, C. (1980).The Nature and Prevalence of Teacher Stress, *Journal of Occupational Psychology,* 21, 27-33.

Laughlin, A. (1984a).Occupational Stress and Its Relationship to Social Supports and Life Turbulence, Unpublished Doctoral Dissertation, University of New Southwales, Australia.

Laughtin, A. (1984b). Teacher Stress in an Australian Setting: The Role of Biographical Mediators.*Educational Study,* 10(1), 7-22.

Lavingia, K.U. (1974). A Study of Job Satisfaction Among School Teachers, *Ph.D. Thesis,* Gujurat University.

Lester, P.E. (1987). Development and Factor Analysis of the Teacher Job Satisfaction Questionnaire (TJSQ), *Educational and Psychological Measurement, 47 (1)*, 223-233

Levin, H.M. (1987). *Towards Accelerated Schools.* Stanford, CA: Stanford University, Centre for Educational Research.

Litt, M.D. & Jurk, D.C. (1985). Sources of Stress and Dissatisfaction in Experiences High School Teachers, *Journal of Educational Research*, 78, 178-185.

Little, J.W. (1982). Norms of Collegiality and Experimentation: Workplace Conditions of School Success. *American Educational Research Journal*, 19, 325-340.

Little, J.W. (1990). Teachers as Colleagues. In A. Lieberman (Ed.), *Schools as Collaborative Cultures: Creating the Future Now.* New York: Falmer.

Littrel, P.C., Billingreley, B.S.& Cross, L.H. (1994).The Effects of Principal Support on Special and General Educators' Stress, Job Satisfaction, School Commitment, Health and Intention to Stay in Teaching, *Remedial and Special Education*, 15, 297-310.

Locke, E.A. (1976). The Nature and Causes of Job Satisfaction. In Dunnette, M.D. (Ed.) *Handbook of Industrial and Organizational Psychology.* (pp. 1297-1349). Chicago: Rand McNally.

Lortie, D.C. (1975). *Schoolteacher: A Sociological Study.* University of Chicago Press.

Louis, K. S. (1998). Effects of Teacher Quality of Work Life in Secondary Schools on Commitment and Sense of Efficacy. *School Effectiveness and School Improvement*, 9(1), pp.1-27.

Lynch, B.P., & Verdin, J.A. (1987). Organisational Commitment: Analysis of Antecedents. *Human Relations 40 (4)*, 219-236.

Malhotra, S., Sruti, & Sachdeva, S. (2001). Work Behaviour and Job Satisfaction: A Study in Banking Industry. *Prestige Journal of Management and Research*, 5(1), 43-48.

Malik, A.K., & Sabharwal, M. (1999). Locus of Control as Determinant of Organizational Role Stress. *Journal of the Indian Academy of Applied Psychology*, 25 (1-2), 61-64.

Manthei, R. & Gilmore, A. (1996). Teacher Stress in Intermediate Schools. *Educational Research*, Vol. 38, No. 1, pp. 3-19

Marr, M. & Mathur, R. K. (1973). Job Satisfaction of Teacher Educators. *Indian Educational Review*, 8 (2).

Margolis, B.L., Kores, W.H. & Quinn, R.P. (1974). Job Stress: An Unlisted Occupational Hazard, *Journal of Occupational Medicine*, 16, 654-661.

Maslach, C. (1982). Understanding Burnout: Definitional Issues in Analyzing a Complex Phenomenon. In Paine, W.S. (Ed.) *Job Stress and Burnout.* (pp. 29-40). Beverly Hills: Sage.

Martin, C. & Stephen, W. (1989).*Teaching and Stress.* Open University Press, USA.

Maslach, C., & Jackson, S.E. (1984). Burnout in Organizational Settings. In S.Oskamp (Ed.), *Applied Social Psychology Annual* (Vol.5). Beverly Hills, CA: Sage.

Mathieu, J.E. & Zajac, D.M. (1990). A Review and Meta Analysis of the Antecedents Correlates and Consequences of Organizational Commitment. *Psychological Bulletin 108*, 171-199.

Mathur, B. S. (1981). Mobility Patterns and Professional Commitment of Higher Secondary Women Teachers of Delhi, *Fourth Survey of Research in Education* (1983-1988), New Delhi: NCERT, Vol. I.

Mathur, P. (1994). Role Stress in Police Officers: An Exploratory Study. *Indian Journal of Criminology*, 22 (1), 9-14.

Mathur, P. (1995). Perceptions of Police Stress: An Empirical Study of Stressors and Coping Responses Among Police Personnel in India.*Indian journal of Criminology*, 23 (1), 9-12.

Mathur, P., Aycan, Z., & Kanungo, N.R. (1996). Work Cultures in Indian Organizations: A Comparison Between Public and Private Sector. Psychology and Developing Societies, 8(2), 199-222.

Mathur, S., & Singhvi, M.K. (1997). Organisational Role Stress. In D.M.Pestonjee (Ed.), *Stress and coping: The Indian Experience* (2nd ed., pp. 87-136). New Delhi: Sage Publication.

McCormick, J. (1997a). Occupational Stress of Teachers: Biographical Differences in a Large School System. *Journal of Educational Administration*, 35 (1), 18-38.

McCormick, J. (1997b). An Attribution Model of Teachers' Occupational Stress and Job Satisfaction in a Large Educational System. *Work and Stress*, 11 (1), 17-32.

McCormick, J. (2000). Psychological Distancing and Teachers' Attribution of Responsibility for Occupational Stress in a Catholic Education System. *Issues in Educational Research*, 10 (1), 55-66.

McCormick, J.& Solman, R. (1992a). The Externalised Nature of Teachers'Occupational Stress and Its Association with Job Satisfaction. *Work and Stress*, 6 (1), 33-44.

McCormick, J. & Solman, R. (1992b). Teachers' Attributions of Responsibility for Occupational Stress and Satisfaction: An Organisational Perspective. *Educational Studies*, 18 (2), 201-222.

Mehra, G. (1993). Group-oriented Attitude as a Moderator Variable of Intrinsic Job Satisfaction-occupational Stress Relationship. *Indian journal of behavior*, 17(3), 13-18.

Mehra, G. & Mishra, P.C. (1993). Participation in Opinion Seeking as a Moderator Variable of Intrinsic Job Satisfaction- occupational Stress Relationship. *Journal of the Indian Academy of Applied Psychology*, 25(1-2), 51-55.

Mercer, D. (1993). Job Satisfaction and the Head Teacher: A Nominal Group Approach. *School Organisation*, 13 (2), 153-164.

Mehra, G. & Mishra, P.C. (1999). Integration of Personality as a Moderator Variable of the Intrinsic Job satisfaction-occupational Stress Relationship. *Journal of the Indian Academy of Applied Psychology*, 25 (1-2), 51-55

Menon, M.E. & Christou, C. (2002). Perceptions of Future and Current Teachers on the Organization of Elementary Schools: A Disonance Approach to the Investigation of Job Satisfaction. *Educational Research*, 44 (1), 97-110.

Metz, M.H. (1988, Aril). *Teachers' Ultimate Dependence on Their Students: Implications for Teachers' Responses to Student Bodies of Differing Social Classes*. Paper Presented at the Annual Meeting of the American Educational Research Association, New Orleans.

Meyer, J.W., & Rowan, B. (1978). The Structure of Educational Organizations. In M. Meyer & Associates (Eds.), *Environments and organizations*. San Francisco: Jossey-Bass.

Meyer, J.P., & Allen, N.J. (1991). A Three Component Conceptualization of Organizational Commitment, *Human Resource Management Review 1*, 61-89.

Meyer, J. P., & Allen, N. J. (1997). Commitment in the Workplace: Theory, Research, and Application. Thousand Oaks, CA: Sage.

Miles, M.B., & Huberman, A.M. (1984). *Qualitative Data Analysis*. Bevery Hills, CA: Sage.

Michael, J. & Dunkin, M. (1987). *The International Encyclopaedia of Teaching and Teacher Education*, The University of Sydney, Australia.

Michailidis, A. (2002). Occupational Stress as It Relates to Higher Education, Individuals and Organisation Work, *Journal of Prevention, Assessment to Rehabilitation*, 19(2), 137-147.

Mishra, K.S. (1993). Teachers and Their Education. Ambala Cants: *The Associate Publisher.*

Mishra, S. (1999).*Teacher Effectiveness of Elementary School Teachers in Relation to Their Attitude Towards Teaching, Level of Aspiration and Job Satisfaction*, Ph.D(Edu.). Kurukshetra University,Haryana.

Mishra, P., Bhardwaj, G., & Mishra, P.K. (1999). Organisational Frustration and Alienation Among Middle Managers. In D.M.Pestonjee, U. Pareek, & R. Agrawal (Eds), *Stress and Its Management* (pp.91-96). New Delhi: Oxford and IBH Publishing Co.

Mishra, P.C. (1995). Role Stress in Special Groups. In D.M.Pestonjee (Ed.), *Stress and Coping: The Indian experience* (2nd ed., pp. 137-215). New Delhi: Sage Publication.

Mishra, P.C., & Somani, H.R. (1993). Occupational Stress in Relation to Mental Health of Supervisors. *Indian Journal of Behaviour*, 17(4), 1-5.

Mishra, P.C., & Srivastava, S. (2000). Role Ambiguity as a Moderator Variable of the Affective Commitment and Job Satisfaction Relationship. *Journal of Community Guidance and Research*, 17 (1), 68-75.

Mishra, P.K., & Bhardwaj, G. (2000). A Study of Perceived Motivational Climate Among Air Traffic Controllers. *Abhigyan*, 18(2), 35-40.

Mishra, P.K., Metha, S., & Bhardwaj, G. (1997). Role Stress in Special Groups. In D.M.Pestonjee (Ed.), *Stress and Coping: The Indian Experience* (2nd ed., pp. 137-215). New Delhi: Sage Publications.

Mishra, M. (1997). Role Stress in Special Groups. In D.M.Pestonjee (Ed.), *Stress and Coping: The Indian Experience* (2nd ed., pp. 137-215). New Delhi: Sage Publications.

Mishra, N. (1998). Stress and Burnout as Related to Social Support in Medical Professions. In Q.H.Gyan (Ed.), *Applied Psychology: Indian Perspective* (pp. 151-158). New Delhi: Gyan Publishing House.

Mital, P. (1995). Role Stress with its Actual and Desired Modes of Conflict Resolution. *Indian Journal of Industrial Relations*, 30 (3), 308-319.

Mohan, V., & Chauhan, D. (1999). A Comparative Study of Organizational Sectors. *Journal of the Indian Academy of Applied Psychology*, 25 (1-2), 45-50.

Mohanty, S.(1992). *Occupational Stress and Mental Health of Executives: A Comparative Study of Public and Private Sector.* M.Phil. (Psy) dissertation, Utkal University.

Mohapatra, C. (1992). *Job Stress, Mental Health and Coping: A Study on Professionals.* M.Phil. (Psychology) Dissertation, Utkal University.

Moriarty, V., Edmonds, S., Blatchford, P. & Martin, C. (2001). Teaching Young Children: Perceived Satisfaction and Stress. *Educational Research*, 43 (1), 33-46.

Morris, J. H. & Sherman, J. D. (1981). Generalizability of an Organizational Commitment Model. *Academy of Management Journal*, Vol.24, pp.512-26

Morris, J. H. & Steers, R. M. (1980). Structural Influences on Organizational Commitment. *Journal of Vocational Behaviour*, Vol.17, pp.50-57.

Mowday, R., Porter, L., & Steers, R. (1982). *Employee-organisation Linkages*. New York: Academic Press.

Mowday, R., Porter, L. & Steers, R. (1979). The Measurement of Organization Commitment. *Journal of Vocational Behaviour*, 14, 224-247

Mowday, R.T. & McDade, T. (1979). Linking behavioural and Attitudinal Commitment: A Longitudinal Analysis of Job Choice and Job Attitudes. In *Proceedings of the 39th Annual Meeting of the Academy of Management*, Atlanta, GA.

Mukherjee, D., & Pestonjee, M.D. (2000). Organisational Change and Perceived Role Efficacy. In O.B.Sayeed & U. Pareek (Eds.), *Actualizing Managerial roles: Studies in Role Efficacy* (pp.193-203). New Delhi: Tata Mc Graw-Hill Publishing Company Limited.

Munt, V. (2004). The Awful Truth: A Micro-history of Teacher Stress at Westwood High. *British Journal of Sociology of Education*, 25 (5), 578-591.

Mykletun, R.J. (1984).Teacher Stress: Perceived and Objective Sources, and Quality of Life, *Scandinavian Journal of Educational Research*, 28 17-45.

Naaz, H. (1999). Job Characteristics and Demographic Variables as Predictors of Job Involvement of Textile Mill Workers. *Journal of the Indian Academy of Applied Psychology*, 25 (1-2), 75-78.

Nazir, A. (1998). A Study of Job Satisfaction of Clerks, *Indian Psychological Abstract and Review*, 10(2), 275.

Nazir, N.A. & Ahmad, S.F. (1998). Sources of Satisfaction and Dissatisfaction Among Teachers. (A Test of Two-factor Theory). *Indian Journal of Training and Development*, 28(4), 19-29.

Nias, J. (1981).Commitment and Motivation in Primary School Teachers. *Educational Review*, 33(3), pp. 181-190.

Nias, J. (1996). Thinking About Feeling: The Emotions in Teaching. *Cambridge Journal of Education*,26(3), pp. 293-306.

Nkereuwem, E.E. (1990). Issues on the Relationship between Job Satisfaction, Job Attitudes and Work Behaviour Among the Staff in Academic Libraries. *Information Services and Use, 10 (5)*, 281-291.

Okebukola, P. A. & Jegede, O. J. (1987). Determinants of Occupational Stress Among Teachers in Nigeria, *Educational Studies*, 15(1), 23-36.

Oldham, G.R. & Hackman, J.R. (1981). Relationships Between Organizational Structure and Employees' Reactions: Comparing Alternative Frameworks. *Administrative Science Quartery*, 26, pp.66-83.

Orpen, C. (1996). Cognitive Failure as a Moderator of the Effect of Work Stress on Personal Strain: An Empirical study. *Psychological Studies*, 41 (1-2), 50-52.

Otto, R. (1982).*Occupational Stress Among Teachers in Post-primary Education: A Study of Teachers in Technical Schools and Some Comparative Data on High School Teachers*, Department of Sociology, Melbourne: La Trobe University.

O'Connor, P.R. & Clarke, V.A. (1990). Determinants of Teacher Stress. *Australian Journal of Education , 34 (1)*, 41-51.

Otto, R. (1986). *Teachers Under Stress: Health Hazards in a Work-Role and Modes of Response.* Melbourne: Hill of Content.

Owner, B. D. (1997). A Study of Factors Affecting Job Satisfaction Among Arkanasas Secondary Principals, *Dissertation Abstract International*, 57 (8) 3346.

Padmanabhaiah, S. (1986). Job Satisfaction and Training Effectiveness. *Ph.D. Thesis*, Sri Venkateswar University.

Padaki, R. (1988). Job Attitudes. In J. Pandey (Ed.), *Psychology in India: The State of the Art* (Vol.3, pp. 19-95). New Delhi: Sage Publications.

Panchanatham, N., Rajendran, K., & Karupplah, K. (1993). Executives' Problem Solving Styles and Occupational Stress, *Journal of Community Guidance and Research*, 10(3), 217-227.

Panda, P. (2001).Job Satisfaction of Dotcom Executives at Various Levels from Content Managers to Vice-Presidents, *Indian Psychological Abstract and Review*, 10(2), 275.

Panda, B. N., Pradhan, N.& Senapathy, H. K. (1996). Job Satisfaction of Secondary Teachers and Relation to Their Mental Health, Age, Sex and Management of School. *Indian Journal of Applied Psychology*. 33(2), 94-100.

Pandey, P. (1986).Organisational Commitment, Professional Commitment and Job Involvement in Relation to the Organisationl Climate, Micro Job Climate and Personality Variables. *Psychological Abstract*; 5(4), 128.

Pandey, A. (1997a). Motivational Analysis of Organizational Behaviour: An Experience with Rail Engine Drivers. *Indian Journal of Industrial Relations*, 33(1), 34-37.

Pandey, A. (1997b). Organizational Role Stress. In D.M.Pestonjee (Ed.), Stress and Coping: The Indian experience (2nd ed., pp. 87-136). New Delhi: Sage Publication.

Pandey, A. (2000). Role Efficacy and Job Performance Measures. In O.B.Sayeed & U. Pareek (Eds), *Actualising Managerial Roles: Studies in Role Efficacy* (pp.184-192). New Delhi: Tata McGraw-Hill Publishing Company Limited.

Pandey, S. C. (1998). A Study of Relationship Between Personality Dimensions and Organizational Role Stress in a Private Sector Organization. *Indian Journal of Industrial Relations*, 33(4), 506-516.

Pant, N., & Bhardwaj, G. (1992). Executive Stress and Its Correlates. *Indian Journal of Industrial Relations*, 27(4), 396-411.

Pareek, U. (1994). Coercive and Persuasive Power Scale. *Indian Journal of Industrial Relations*. 30(2), 175-189.

Patel, K.M. (1999a). A Study of Impact of Age on Job Involvement and Organizational Commitment of Nationalized and Cooperative Bank Employees. *Journal of the Indian Academy of Applied Psychology*, 25 (1-2), 65-70.

Patel, K.M. (1999b). Differences in HRD Climate, Organizational Climate, Job Satisfaction and Job Involvement Between High and Low Performing Branches of DCCBs. In C. Balaji & P.K.Reddy (Eds), *Organisational Behaviour Issues in Rural Co-operatives* (pp.264-265). New Delhi: Allied Publishers Ltd.

Pattnaiak, R. (2002). Effects of Shift Work and Hierarchical Position in the Organisational Psychological Correlates: A Study on an Integrated Steel Plant, *Psychological Abstract*, 5(8), 1235.

Pattanayak, B., & Mishra, P.K. (1997a). Explore Prevalence and Determinants of Organizational Climate, Job Stress and Job Strain Among Service Sector Employees. In B. Pattanayak & P.K.Mishra (Eds), *Life in Organisations* (pp.196-218). New Delhi: Wheeler Publishing.

Pattanayak, B., & Mishra, P.K. (1997b). Extent to Which Individual Attributes and Organizational Characteristics Contribute or Influence in Developing a Sense of Organizational Commitment. In B.Pattanayak & P.K.Mishra(Eds),*Life in Organisations* (pp.196-218). New Delhi: Wheeler Publishing.

Pattanayak, B., Panda, K.P., & Mohapatra, K.J. (1999). Job Stress and Organizational Commitment. In D.M.Pestonjee, U. Pareek, & R.Agarwal (Eds), *Studies in stress and Its Management* (pp.61-71). New Delhi:Oxford and IBH Publishing Co.

Pestonjee, D.M. (1995). Role-stress in Special Groups. In D.M.Pestonjee (Eds.), *Stress and Coping: The Indian experience* (2nd ed., pp.137-215). New Delhi: Sage Publications.

Porter, L.,Crampon, W.,& Smith, F. (1976). *Organisational Behaviour and Human Performance*, 15, 87-98.

Porter, L. W., Steers, R. M., Mowday, R.T. & Boulian, P. (1974). Organisational Commitment, Job-satisfaction and Turnover Among Psychiatric Technicians. *Journal of Applied psychology*,59, 603-609.

Pradhan, M., & Khatri, P.K. (2001). Intrapsychic and Extrapsychic Predictors of Burnout in Doctors: Gender Differences. *Journal of Community Guidance and Research*, 18(2), 129-136.

Purkey, S.C., & Smith, M.S. (1983). Effective Schools: A Review. *Elementary School Journal*, 83, 427-452.

Purohit, S., & Pareek, U. (2000). Development of Role Efficacy Scale for Nurses. In O.B.Sayeed & U.Pareek (Eds), *Actualising Managerial Roles: Studies in Role Efficacy* (pp.45-49). New Delhi: Tata McGraw Hill Publishing Company Limited.

Punch, K.F. & Tuetteman, E. (1996). Reducing Teacher Stress: The Effects of Support in the Work Environment. *Research in Education*, 56, 63-72.

Quinn, R.P., & Staines, G.L. (1979). *The 1977 Quality of Employment Survey*. Ann Arbor:University of Michigan, Institute for Social Research.

Raj, S., & Sinha, A.K. (2000). Transformational Leadership, Organizational Commitment and Facilitating Climate. *Psychological Studies*, 45(1&2), 33-42.

Raj, T. (2001). An Empirical Study of Correlates of Teacher Effectiveness of Secondary School Teachers. *The Educational Review*, 107 (1), 6-8

Rajeswari, T.R. (1992). Employee Stress: A Study with Reference to Bank Employees. *Indian journal of Industrial Relations*, 27(4), 419-429.

Raju, M.V.R., & Madhu, K. (1994). Organisational Level and Role Stress. *Journal of Indian Psychology*, 12(1-2), 62-66.

Ramakrishnaih, D. (1989). Job Satisfaction of College Teachers. *Ph.D Thesis*, Sri Venkateswar University.

Rana, S. (1981).Professional Commitment of Home Science College Teachers in India and Its Relationship to Personal and Professional Characteristics and to Organisational Climate. *Fourth Survey of Research in Education* (1983-1988). New Delhi: NCERT, Vol.I.

Rani Lakshmi, D., & Mishra, K.P. (2001). Occupational Stress Among Working Women in Emergence Services. *Management and Labour Studies*, 26(1), 25-36.

Rutebuks, A.K. (1997). Job Satisfaction of Teachers in Seventh-day Adentist Schools and Its Relationship to Commitment and Selected Work Condition. *Dissertation Abstract International*, 57 (7) 2787.

Rawat, S. (1992). A Study of the Expectations and Realities of Job, Job Satisfaction and Value Pattern of Secondary School Teachers in Relation to Their Sex. *Ph.D. Thesis*, Rohilkhand University.

Ray, E.B. & Miller, K.I. (1991). The Influence of Communication Structure and Social Support on Job Stress and Burnout. *Management Communication Quarterly*, 4 (4), 506-527.

Rao, S. N. (1986). *Work Adjustment and Job-satisfaction of Teachers*. Mittal Publications, Delhi-35.

Riketta, S. (2002).Attitudinal Organisational Commitment and Job Performance: A Meta-analysis.*Psychological Abstract*, 3, 123.

Reddy, B.P. (1989). Job Satisfaction of Primary School Teacher. *M.Phil Thesis*, Sri Venkateswara University.

Reddy, C.T., Gajendran, M. & Gayathri, S. (2000). Organisational Climate and Dual Commitment in Private and Public Sector Enterprises. *Indian Journal of Industrial Relations*, 36(1), 53-66.

Reddy, V.S., & Ramamurti, P.V. (2000). The Relation Between Stress Experience on the Job: Age, Personality and General Ability. *Psychological Studies*, 36(2), 87-95

Rishi, P., Sinha, S.P., & Dubey, R. (2000). A Co-relational Study of Workplace Characteristics and Work Satisfaction Among Indian Bank Employees. Psychologia: *An International Journal of Psychology in the Orient*, 43(3), 155-164.

Rose, M. (2003).Good Deal, Bad Deal? Job Satisfaction in Occupations. Work, Employment and Society, 17(3), 503-30

Rosenblatt, Z. & Shirom, A. (2005). Predicting Teacher Absenteeism by Personal Background Factors. *Journal of Educational Administration*, 43 (2), 209-225.

Roy, A. (1997). Executive Stress and Social Support: An Exploratory Study. *Abhigyan*, 15(4), 25-31.

Rusbult F. (1983). Commitment and Its Theoretical Determinants: A Meta-analysis of the Investment Models. *Personal Relationships*, 10(1), 37-57.

Russell, D. W., Altmaier, E., & Van Velzen, D. (1987). Job-related Stress, Social Support, and burnout. *Journal of Applied Psychology*, 72, 269-274.

Saran,M. (2001). *Census of India* Series-22, Director of Census Operation, Orissa.

Sarma, M.S.R. (1991). A Study of the Administrative Behaviour of Principals as Perceived by Teachers in Relation to Job Satisfaction of Teachewrs and Students' Achievement in junior college. *Ph.D Thesis*, Andhra University.

Sarros, J.C. & Sarros, A.M. (1992). Social Support and Teacher Burnout. *Journal of EducationalAdministration*, 30 (1), 55-69.

Sahoo, F.M., Mohanty, A., & Bhakat, M. (1995). Role Stress in Employees of Administrative and Financial Organizations. *The Creative Psychologist*, 7(1-2), 23- 32.

Schonfeld, I. S. (1990a). Coping with Job-related Stress: The Case of Teachers. *Journal of Occupational Psychology*, 63, 141-149.

Sergiovanni, T. (1967). Factors Which Affect Satisfaction and Dissatisfaction of Teachers. *Journal of Educational Administration*, 5 pp.66-81.

SCMP Issue in 1990, *South China Morning Post*, Hong Kong.

Scott, C., Cox, S. & Dinham, S. (1999). The Occupational Motivation, Satisfaction and Health of English School Teachers. *Educational Psychology*, 19 (3), 287-308.

Scott, C. & Dinham, S. (2003). The Development of Scales to Measure Teacher and School Executive Occupational Satisfaction. *Journal of Educational Administration*, 41 (1), 74-86.

Scott, C., Stone, B. & Dinham, S. (2001). I Love Teaching But ... International Patterns of Discontent'. Educational Policy Archives, 9(28).Online at: http://epaa.asu.edu/epaa/v9n28.html

Sekaran, U. (1989). *Organizational Behaviour: Text and Cases*, Tata McGraw-Hill, New Delhi.

Selye, H. (1974). *Stress Without Distness*, London: Hodder and Stoughton.

Selye,H. (1956). *The Stress of Life*, New York: McGraw Hill.

Shann, M. (1998). Professional Commitment and Satisfaction Among Teachers in Urban Middle Schools. *Journal of Educational Research*, 92, 67—73.

Shore, L.M., & Wagner, S.J. (1993). Commitment and Employees Behaviour. Comparison of Affective Commitment with Perceived Organizational Support. *Journal of Applied Psychology* , 78, 774-780.

Singh, D. (1974). Job Satisfaction and Job Behaviour. *Indian Psychological Abstract*, 5 (3)

Singh, N. (1991).The Effect of Organisational Role Stress, Organisational Climate and Locus of Control on the Job Involvement of Bank Employees .*Indian Educational Abstract*, 1(4), 43.

Singh, O. & Singh, R. (1998). Job Stress Among Secondary School Teachers in Relation to Management, Six and Marital Status. *Indian Educational Abstract*. 5(8), 57.

Sanghi, S. (2001). A Study of Motivational Climate in Relation to Job Satisfaction and Organizational Commitment. *Journal of Foundation of Organizational Research and Education*, 19(1), 19- 25.

Singh, K. & Billingsley, B.S. (1996). Intent to Stay in Teaching: Teachers of Students with Emotional Disorders *vs.* Other Special Eductors. *Remedial and SpecialEducation*, 17 (1), 37-47.

Singh, K. & Billingsley, B.S. (1996). Professional Support and Its Effects on Teachers' Commitment. *The Journal of Educational Research*, 91(4), 229-239.

Smith, R. W. (1997). Participatory Decision Making, Job Satisfaction and Teacher Absenteeism in Selected Florida Middle School, *Dissertation Abstract International*, 54(10), 4217.

Smith, M. & Burke, S. (1992). Teacher Stress: Examining a Model Based on Context, Workload and Satisfaction. *Teaching and Teacher Education*, 8 (1), 31-46.

Snape & Kirk, M. (2002). An Evaluation of a Three Component Model of Occupational Commitment: Dimensionality and Consequences Among United Kingdom Human Resource Management Specialists. *Psychological Abstract*, 2, 125.

Solman, R. & Feld, M. (1989). Occupational Stress: Perceptions of Teachers in Catholic Schools. *Journal of Educational Administration, 27 (3)*, 55-68.

Spector, P.E. (2000). *Industrial and Organizational Psychology: Research and Practice* (2nd ed.). New York: John Wiley & Sons.

Srivastav, S. (1986). A Study of Job Satisfaction and Professional Honesty of Primary School Teachers with Necessary Suggestions. Ph.D.Thesis. Agra University.

Srivastava, A.K. (1989).Moderating Effect on self Actualization on the Relationship of Role Stress with Job Anxiety. *Psychological Studies*, 34(2) 107-111.

Starnaman, S.M. & Miller, K.I. (1992). A Test of a Causal Model of Communication and Burnout in the Teaching Profession. *Communication Education*, 41 (1), 40-55.

Steers, R. M. (1977). Antecedent and Outcomes of Organizational Commitment *Administrative Science Quarterly*. 22, 46-56.

Steers, R.M. & Rhodes, S.R. (1978). Major Influences on Employee Attendance: A Process Model. *Journal of Applied Psychology*.63, pp.391-407

Stenlund, K.V. (1995). Teacher Perceptions Across Cultures: The Impact of Students on Teacher Enthusiasm and Discouragement in a Cross-cultural Context. *The Alberta Journal of Educational Research*, 41 pp.145-61.

Stingthamber, C, T. (2003). Organizations and Supervisors as Sources of Support and Targets of Commitment: as Sources of Support and Targets of Commitment—A Longitudinal Study, *Psychological Abstract*, 3, 1233.

Sudhira (1996). Teacher Job Satisfaction and Job Stress of Secondary School Physical Education Teachers Working in Different Management Schools in Madhya Pradesh. *Indian Educational Abstract*, 1, 47.

Summers, T.P., DeCotiis, T.A. & DeNisi, A.S. (1995). A Field Study of Some Antecedents and Consequences of Felt Job Stress. In Crandall, R. and Perrewe, P.L. (Ed.s) *Occupational Stress: A Handbook*. (pp. 113-128). Washington D.C.: Taylor & Francis.

Tahira, K. (2000). Job Satisfaction of Secondary School Teachers in Relation to Their Personal Variables Sex, Experience, Professional Training, Salary and Religion. *Indian Educational Abstract*, (7&8) 97.

Teo, C. (2002).The Role of Human Resource Practices in Reading Occupational Stress and Strain. *Psychological Abstract*, 5, 69.

Thanagosai, S. (1990). Job Satisfaction Among Faculty Members at Six Metropolitan Area Teachers College in Bangkok, Thailand. *Dissertation Abstract International*, 50 (7).

Thomas, N., Clarke, V. & Lavery, J. (2003). Self-reported Work and Family Stress of Female Primary Teachers. *Australian Journal of Education*, 47 (1), 73-87.

Thomas, P., Dose, J. & Scott, K. S. (2002), Relationship Between Accountability, Job Satisfaction and Trust. *Human Resource Development Quarterly*, 13(3), 307-323.

Tollenback, S., Brenner, S., & Lofgren, H. (1983). Teacher Stress: Exploratory Model Building. *Journal of Occupational Psychology, 56*, 19-33.

Troman, G. (2000). Teacher Stress in the Low Trust Society. *British Journal of Sociology of Education*, 21 (3), 331-353.

Travers, C. J. & Cooper, C. L. (1996). Teacher Under Pressure: Stress in the Teaching Profession. *European Review of Applied Psychology*, 46, 102-128.

Troman, G. & Woods, P. (2000).Careers Under Stress: Teacher Adaptations at a Time of Intensive Reform, *Journal of Educational Change*, Vol. 1 pp.253-75.

Trendall, C. (1989). Stress in Teaching and Teacher Effectiveness: A Study of Teachers Across Mainstream and Special Education. *Educational Research, 31*(1), 52-58.

Tshannen-Moran, M., Woolfolk-Hoy, A. & Hoy, W. (1998). Teacher Efficacy: Its Meaning and Measure,*Review of Educational Research*, Vol. 68 pp.202-48.

Tsui, K. T., & Cheng, Y. C. (1999). School Organisational Health and Teacher Commitment: A Contingency Study with Multi-level Analysis. *Educational Research and Evaluation*, 5(3), 249-268.

Tyree, A. K. (1996). Conceptualising and Measuring Commitment to High School Teaching. *Journal of Educational Research*, 89(5), pp. 295-304.

Upadhyay, B. & Singh, B. (2001). Occupational stress among college and school teachers, *Indian Educational Abstract*, 1(1-2), 20.

Vagg, R., Spielberger, C. D. & Wasala, C. F. (2002).Effects of Organizational Level and Gender on Stress in the Workplace," *International Journal of Stress Management*, 9(4), 243-261

Van Scotter, J.R. (2000). Relationships of Task Performance and Contextual Performance with Turnover, Job Satisfaction and Affective Commitment. *Human Resources Management Review*, 10(1), 79-95.

Vroom, V.H. (1964). *Work and Motivation*. New York: John Wiley & Sons.

Weiss, H.M. (2002). Deconstructing Job Satisfaction: Separating Evaluations, Beliefs and Affective Experiences *Human Resources Management Review*, 12(2), 173-94.

Whitehead, A.J. & Ryba, K. (1995). New Zealand Teachers' Perceptions of Occupational Stress and Coping Strategies. *New Zealand Journal of Educational Studies*, 30 (2), 177-188.

Wright, B.E. & Davis, B.S. (2001).' Job Satisfaction in the Public Sector: The Role of the Work Environment '. American Review of Public Administration, 33(1), 70-90.

Wisniewski, R.G. (1997).Occupational Stress and Burnout Among Special Educators: A Review of the Literature. *The Journal of Special Education*, 31(3), 325-346

Wood, P. (1992). Symbolic Interactionism: Theory and Method. In M. D. LeCompte & W. L. Millroy & J. Preissle (Eds.), *The Handbook of Qualitative Research in Education*. San Diego: Academic Press, Inc.

Woods, A.M. & Weasmer, J. (2004). Maintaining Job Satisfaction: Engaging Professionals as Active Participants. *Clearing House*, 77 (3), 118-136.

Yousef, D. A.C. (2002). Job-satisfaction as a Mediator of the Relationship Between Role Stressors and Organizational Commitment: A study from an Arabic Cultural Perspective, *Journal of Managerial Psychology*, Vol. 17(4), pp. 250-266.

Yong, B. C. (1999). The career commitment of Primary Teachers in Brunei Darussalam: Perceptions of teaching as a career. *Research in Education* (62), pp.1-7. DEN05203.

Yue, X. D. (1995, March). *A Study of Occupational Stress Among Primary and Secondary Schools Guidance Teachers in Hong Kong*. Paper presented at the Faculty Research Seminar at the Chinese University of Hong Kong.

Zembylas, M. & Papanastasiou, E. (2004). Job Satisfaction Among School Teachers in Cyprus. *Journal of Educational Administration* , 42(3), 357-74.

Index